Open access edition supported by the National Endowment for the Humanities /
Andrew W. Mellon Foundation Humanities Open Book Program.

© 2019 Johns Hopkins University Press
Published 2019

Johns Hopkins University Press
2715 North Charles Street
Baltimore, Maryland 21218-4363
www.press.jhu.edu

ISBN-13: 978-1-4214-3399-8 (open access)
ISBN-10: 1-4214-3399-0 (open access)

ISBN-13: 978-1-4214-3397-4 (pbk. : alk. paper)
ISBN-10: 1-4214-3397-4 (pbk. : alk. paper)

T0385576

ISBN-13: 978-1-4214-3398-1 (electronic)
ISBN-10: 1-4214-3398-2 (electronic)

This page supersedes the copyright page included in the original publication of this work.

THE INDIVIDUAL
AND SOCIETY
IN THE MIDDLE AGES

In 1963 the Humanities Group at The Johns Hopkins University initiated a five-year series of graduate seminars devoted to the study of a particular period or topic. These are designed to bring to the campus distinguished visiting scholars and are open to graduate students, post-doctoral fellows, and faculty members.

As a part of this program, the 1964–65 Mediaeval Seminars concentrated on the period of the Middle Ages and brought to the University Walter Ullmann, who conducted his seminar in "Problems of Social and Political Theory." This, like other seminars in the series, was paralleled by the teaching of related graduate courses.

THE INDIVIDUAL
AND SOCIETY
IN THE MIDDLE AGES

Walter Ullmann

THE JOHNS HOPKINS PRESS
BALTIMORE, MARYLAND

To the Memory of
SIDNEY PAINTER

PREFACE

When during my tenure as visiting professor of humanistic studies at The Johns Hopkins University I was invited to give some public lectures, I accepted the undeserved honor and privilege with alacrity. This gave me an excellent opportunity to put before a larger—and, as it turned out, a most appreciative—audience the results of some of my research. In several respects the invitation was also a challenge, especially insofar as I was forced to clarify my own thoughts upon a topic which has engaged my attention for a number of years and on which I could do no more than touch in some of my recent publications.

Looking as a medievalist at the modern and contemporary period and its rather bulky output on the topic of the individual and society, I have long been struck by the total absence of any historical treatment of this topic. This lacuna seems to me all the more noteworthy since there is virtually no other subject or topic or problem in the Middle Ages about which historical research has not been conducted. The most minute and, as often as not, quite insignificant questions in medieval history have been subjected to rigorous and repeated examinations, but a theme as central as that of the individual and his standing in medieval society has

not, to all seeming, attracted much attention either among
professional medievalists or among numerous research students. There is, of course, an abundance of historical literature on such politological questions as the rights and
functions of kings, popes, and emperors; on the origin, scope,
and contents of these rights; on medieval representative
bodies; on the legislative process; and the like, but the individual as such—who after all was at all times the center
of things—is only mentioned in passing. Part of the explanation for this lack of *ex professo* treatment may well lie in
the very character of the medieval writings themselves,
which explicitly devoted remarkably little, if any, space to
the standing of the individual, his functions, his rights, his
duties, and so on. Medieval writings dealt, on the other
hand, rather fully with the former topics which are presented to the modern reader by way of classification, system-
atization, division and subdivision, but of the individual
himself one reads extraordinarily little.

There is nowadays considerable attention paid to the
nature of political obligation and related questions—political
scientists no less than sociologists, social psychologists, de-
mographers, and others busy themselves to find the substance
and kernel of this obligation. It is indeed a legitimate source
of inquiry which should have provoked the historians of
medieval political ideas to similar investigations, such as why
medieval man obeyed a king or a pope, why obedience could
be exacted from medieval man, why the latter's right to
advocate heterodox opinions was severely restricted, why,
above all, the individual was, for the greater part of the
Middle Ages, merely a subject and not a citizen, why there
was to be in the course of time a replacement of the subject
by the citizen, with consequences and repercussions still
only dimly grasped. These and similar questions should long
have been the proper métier of historical jurisprudence or
of the historian of political ideas.

At least one potent reason for the neglect of this topic appears to be inattention to linguistic usage. Although medieval writings do not delve explicitly into the standing of the individual, they nevertheless have a great deal to say implicitly on his rights and functions, and so on. Modern research into medieval politology apparently has not yet recognized that a sharp, basic, and conceptual distinction has to be drawn between the individual as a subject and the individual as a citizen. However vital and fundamental it is to discern clearly between these two notions, the distinction has not yet, to my knowledge, excited the interest of modern writers on medieval politological questions. What strikes the attentive reader is that in modern works which should have examined the topic, there is lack of discrimination where subtle discrimination is called for. As soon as the distinction between the notions of the subject and the citizen is realized, however, one is able to test medieval writings and medieval sources adequately, and one soon comes to realize that in medieval doctrine the subject—or for that matter, later, the citizen—occupied a considerable space. To be sure, there was rarely a chapter heading professedly dealing with the topic, and the inquiring historian has, so to speak, to construct, if not to reconstruct the theme, but the thing itself, the subject matter, was there. Moreover, since there was no political science before the thirteenth century, a number of sources must be subjected to close scrutiny, sources which range from the Bible to chancery practices, from law to theology, from liturgy to coronation symbolism, from a theological *Summa* to a publicistic tract, and so on: they all in one way or another have something to say on the individual either as a subject or as a citizen.

What I intended to do in these three lectures was no more than to direct attention to this vital problem of the subject and of the citizen, and to delineate the process by which the latter supplanted the former. In trying to indicate the main phases by which this process of replacement took place, I had to give appropriate space to medieval feudalism which, despite its variegated character in different regions and countries, had nevertheless a number of features which could well be classed as invariable, of whatever kind particular feudal arrangements might have been. It has seemed to me for some time that medieval feudalism contributed at least as much to the growth of specific political ideas as did the learned disquisitions of medieval schoolmen and jurists. This realization of mine owes a great deal to the works of the late Sidney Painter. I considered it, therefore, a very special distinction to be able to give these lectures in Painter's own university, for in this most suitable place I was privileged to propound, with however many shortcomings, the crucial role which feudalism played in the transition from the individual as a subject to a full-fledged citizen, that is, in the transition from medieval to modern times. To dedicate the printed lectures to the memory of Sidney Painter seems to me a self-evident and pleasant duty—it was he who had seen in medieval feudalism one of the great creative forces of the civilization which we like to call modern.

Although historical in content and scope, the problems treated in these lectures also have a certain topical and contemporary-modern interest, for it would be too facile to assume that the properly medieval viewpoint of the individual as a mere subject is of concern only to the professional historian of the Middle Ages. There are still a number of societies and governments today or in the recent past which extol the duty of obedience as the foremost civic virtue, although the citizen has little opportunity of creating and shaping the law which he is to obey. This kind of existence is, from the individual's standpoint, admittedly a comfortable one because it relieves him of making any critical assessments and of forming his own judgment, moving from rationalization to conformity and producing, eventually, uniformity. This obediential standpoint provides a protective shelter for the individual, though he thereby is exposed to the danger of losing what Dante called the most precious gift which God had conferred on man—his freedom. Names and nomenclatures may have changed, but in some structures of modern society one finds, when one approaches it with a critical-historical eye, considerable remnants of the medieval structure of society and of the standing of the individual within it. The emancipation from medieval ways of reasoning and thinking—though they are no longer called by their proper names—has certainly not gone so far as one might be inclined, perhaps unreflectingly, to think. If these lectures were to contribute to a better understanding of the genesis of modern society and the individual within it or at least to open the one or the other vista not hitherto perceived, they might contribute to the realization of the age-old demand γνῶθι σεαυτόν.

The three lectures, delivered at The Johns Hopkins University in March, 1965, are here published in somewhat expanded form. Some of the main conclusions reached formed also the subject of my Frederick Whiton Lecture in the Humanities at Cornell University in May, 1965. In view of the magnitude of the problem, I am fully aware of the work which still needs to be done, but I believe a beginning ought to be made. I have tried, therefore, to fix attention upon some of the salient features, knowing well that even they are in need of supplementation, quite apart from the numerous subordinate and side issues. I have also tried to keep the footnote apparatus to tolerable dimensions and have quoted *in extenso* only where the point required full citation. I thought it right to preserve the structure of the lectures as originally given.

There remains for me only the agreeable duty of thanking the many faculty members of The Johns Hopkins University, especially of the departments of history and of political science, for the stimulating suggestions they made to me and the encouragement I received from them. I would also like to take the opportunity of thanking the alert members of the Humanities Seminar of The Johns Hopkins University for their sometimes searching, sometimes constructive, but always well-informed criticisms which in true scholarly fashion they offered me and which made me realize a number of points to which I might otherwise have paid less attention.

Cambridge   W.U.
November 29, 1965

CONTENTS

THE INDIVIDUAL
AND SOCIETY
IN THE MIDDLE AGES

I

THE ABSTRACT THESIS

The Ecclesiological and Corporational
Theme of Subject and Society

There are probably few topics in modern social and political thought which arouse greater interest than the status, function, and power of the individual within the State, within the organized body of citizens. Although it would be too optimistic to say that the problem has been satisfactorily solved everywhere, there is, nonetheless, at least within the Western orbit, a fairly general agreement on the autonomous, independent status of the individual within society. I think I am right in saying that since the eighteenth century it has become a more or less universally accepted point of view that man as an individual has certain inalienable rights which no power of government can take away and with which no government may with impunity interfere; and further, that as a matter of fact no less than as a matter of doctrine, the individual's participation in government—provided that certain requirements of a formal nature are fulfilled—is his undoubted right; that, in other words, the abstract notion of the State is in reality nothing else but the concrete aggregate of the individual citizens. Hand in hand with this go what are called individual liberties which it would be tedious to enumerate before this forum.

Man's present status is taken so much for granted that it is difficult to realize that it was not always so, that the emergence of the individual within society as its full, autonomous, and constituent member was the result of weary and protracted conflicts which in some respects have not everywhere reached their end. In inviting you to follow

3

me on a historical exploration of the Middle Ages, I am fully conscious not only of the great responsibility which, with inadequate means at my disposal, I, perhaps rashly, have taken upon myself, but also of the delicate nature of the subject itself, especially in view of the brittle state of research on this topic. I derive some comfort, however, if comfort it be, from the fact that there is hardly any modern literature on the topic of the individual and society in the Middle Ages. This, no doubt, is a salutary reminder which is only apt to underline the difficulties and to emphasize the pitfalls confronting me in opening what is virtually virgin soil. And yet, it cannot surely be denied that the European Middle Ages constitute the period in which the basic doctrines affecting the relations between the individual, society, and its government were formulated and applied to an extent which is certainly remarkable.

Considering the intellectual effort that is presently still spent upon the presentation of many already well-trodden medieval topics; reflecting upon the zeal and single-mindedness with which historically quite inessential, if not trivial, matters of medieval history are often pursued by the antiquarians posing as historians; contemplating, further, the great mental labors which go into the transcription, let alone the edition, of medieval manuscripts and the works they contain which add, as often as not, extremely little to our knowledge or better understanding of the historical process itself—one is indeed forcefully struck by the absence of all recognition of the topic which forms the subject of these lectures. This topic is to me, at least from a wider historical angle, a crucial and fundamental one and also a topic of perennial interest, if only for the sake of a better understanding and a more adequate appreciation of the forces which, first, gave the medieval period its character and complexion, and, secondly, potently shaped and influenced modern relevant conceptions.

It seems to me—and I would like to stress the point—that the historical recognition of the vital difference between the individual as a mere subject and the individual as a citizen is long overdue. The two conceptions, subject and citizen, reflect and epitomize in an almost classical and certainly impressionable manner the basic standing of the individual in the public sphere. The recognition of this distinction would seem to further not only the historical-political understanding but also—and perhaps even more so—an appreciation of the ideological forces which in their turn produced these concepts. In a rough sense one may well say that for the larger part of the Middle Ages it was the individual as a subject that dominated the scene, while in the later Middle Ages and in the modern period the subject was gradually supplanted by the citizen. Why was this so? Why did the subject in the high Middle Ages stand in the foreground, and what forces were at work which replaced him by the citizen?

I cannot promise you a cut and dried answer to all the multifarious problems which these questions, in themselves quite simple, pose, but what I intend to do is to invite your attention to some specific medieval conceptions so as to throw the contrast, and herewith the subsequent development, into the clearest possible relief. Looking at the medieval scene from a broad point of view, I find that the topic divides itself quite naturally into three different compartments. There was, first, the purely doctrinal and intellectual standpoint which, for understandable reasons, was the point of view held by those who set the tone and gave the medieval period its particular complexion, that is, by those who attempted to translate the Christian theme into the workaday world, an attempt made by the pronouncedly theocratic governments and writers in the earlier part of the Middle Ages. To this I will devote my first lecture.

There is, secondly, the theme which—with some notable

exceptions—has not been accorded the attention which is surely its due, that is, the feudal complexion of society and the concomitant view of the individual within feudal society. It seems to me impossible to exaggerate the fructifying significance of the feudal theme, precisely in respect of my topic, for within its precincts we do not move in the higher regions of speculative doctrine, dogma, and authority, but keep our gaze firmly fixed on the concrete, mundane, and earthly activities of contemporary, that is, medieval society.

In my third lecture I propose to show that, as a result of the potent fertilization of the ground by feudalism and other agencies not directly linked with political ideology but at least indirectly impinging upon it, new ideas emerged with fructifying effects in the public field. I hope to demonstrate that the new ideas concerning the individual and his standing within society could and did in fact combine and fuse to give birth to a full-fledged humanism, to provide the release of the individual from the tutelage in which he had been kept for so long a time. This is the dawn of the modern era in which the citizen had won the victory over the subject, the era in which the individual was liberated and emancipated.

My first lecture, therefore, will be an attempt to answer the question of why, doctrinally, in the medieval period the individual had not yet emerged as a fully grown citizen, that is, as someone who had in the public field autonomous, independent, and indigenous rights and was entitled to take part in public government itself. In trying to answer this question I am afraid I shall have to ask you to follow me over the somewhat arid and barren ground of some medieval religious and ecclesiological matters, because it seems to me that without at least putting these matters into their proper focus one cannot hope to understand the properly medieval point of view nor the subsequent development.

We must set out from the incontrovertible fact that for

the greater part of the Middle Ages ideas relating to the public sphere were shaped partly by Roman concepts and notions and partly by Christian doctrines. The concepts of Roman parentage which are directly relevant are those concerned with the structure of society as a corporation. This corporational element seems to me a crucial and vital feature of medieval society and has particular relevance to my topic, for in combination with the ecclesiological strain of thought it led without great effort to the thesis that the Christian was a member of the all-embracing, comprehensive corporation, the Church.[1] The incorporation of the Christian into the Church, his becoming a full member of the *corpus Christi*, was effected by his baptism.

Now baptism was not, as one might be inclined to think, merely a liturgical or a sacramental act: to be sure, it was this, too, but within the field of public government, it assumed additional significance that is by no means fully appreciated. The sacramental act of baptism was also endowed with effects in the public field since as a baptized Christian the individual was said to have become a new creature, was said to have undergone a metamorphosis—he ceased to be a mere man; he ceased to be, to use Pauline language, a man of nature, a man of flesh, an "animalic man."[2] As a result of the working of divine grace, he had divested himself of his natural humanity, his *humanitas*,[3] and had become a participant of the divine attributes them-

[1] See Melchiorre Roberti in *Studi in onore di Enrico Besta* (Milan, 1939), IV, 37–82; Arnold Ehrhardt, "Das Corpus Christi und die Corporation im spät-römischen Recht," *Savigny Zeitschrift, Roman. Abt.*, LXX (1953), 299–347, and LXXI (1954), 25ff.

[2] See I Cor. 2:14 and 3:3; Gal. 5:24; Col. 2:12.

[3] See, for instance, Rom. 6:19: "*Humanum* dico propter infirmitatem *carnis* vestrae." It is highly significant that this passage also gave birth to an entirely different interpretation which, coming as it did from so great an authority as Gregory the Great, exercised considerable influence. See Gregory I *Moralia* xi. 49. 65 (Jacques Paul Migne, *Patrologia Latina* lxxv. 982): "Homo natus ex infirmitate, quia de muliere ortus." *Patrologia Latina* is hereafter cited as *Patr. Lat.*

selves. I think one can speak of a renaissance, of a rebirth, because, to use Pauline language again, man emerged as a *nova creatura*:[4] he was *renatus*, was reborn. In view of the later development it is important to bear in mind this concept of a renaissance, for which the New Testament itself can be called upon as a witness.[5] This status of being reborn was also expressed by the metaphysical use of resurrection or of a *regeneratio* or *renovatio*.[6] No doubt, the *glossa ordinaria* on the Bible exegetically paraphrased the gist of the relevant biblical statements by saying that "*Renascitur* homo ex aqua." In this context we should take due note of the tension amounting to a dichotomy which, on the basis of this idea of rebirth, was held to exist between man's natural being, his *humanitas,* and his being as a Christian who moved, so to speak, on a level different from that of his naturalness. The concept of *humanitas* became equated with the merely carnal, the main reason being to bring into clearer relief the contrast to the elevated status of the Christian himself. Thus, Gregory the Great declared that Scripture itself denoted by the collective term *humanitas* the occupation with carnal matters.[7]

This is not merely a doctrinal point of view but also one with fundamental repercussions in the public sphere, for

[4] II Cor. 5:17; Gal. 6:15.

[5] See, for instance, John 3:3–5, which deals with the physical birth and metaphysical rebirth. How, it is here asked, can an old man be reborn? Is he supposed to enter his mother's womb again to be reborn? See further I Pet. 1:23. It may well be that the modern canon law of the Roman Church still adheres to this same principle when it declares (can. 87) that "through baptism man becomes a person"—natural man, as it were, is transformed or reborn into a full person, which he was not before baptism.

[6] See, for example, Titus 3:5. The same idea was expressed by Augustine when he declared that baptism turned its recipient from a mere slave into a son of the great paterfamilias: *Miscellanea Agostiniana,* Vol. I: *Sancti Augustini Sermones post Maurinos reperti* (Rome, 1930), p. 418, ll. 3–11.

[7] See Gregory I *Moralia* xviii. 54. 92 (*Patr. Lat.* lxxvi. 94): "Scriptura quippe sacra omnes carnalium sectatores, *humanitatis* nomine notare solet," referring to I Cor. 3:3, 4.

as a Christian the individual was held to stand on a level quite different from that of a mere man. Not only did he become a member of the Church, but he was also designated as a *fidelis*, with the important consequence that the individual no longer was considered to have shaped his life in accordance with his natural, human insight, a fact which in theory and practice meant that he no longer was endowed with autonomous, indigenous functions insofar as they related to the management of public affairs. As a member of the corporation, of the Church, the *fidelis* was now subjected, as far as his social and public life went, to the law as it was *given* to him, not the law as it was made by him. The consequence of the incorporation was that his *fidelitas*, his faithfulness, consisted precisely in his obeying the law of those who were instituted *over* him by divinity. The individual became absorbed in and by the corporation itself, by the Church, which itself, however, was governed on the monarchic principle, according to which original power was located in one supreme authority, from which all power in the public sphere was derived—a system which, for want of a better name, I call the descending or theocratic theme of government and law.[8]

[8] For some details see Walter Ullmann, *Principles of Government and Politics in the Middle Ages* (London, 1961), pp. 20ff. It should perhaps be noted that the concept of papal monarchy was also constructed by means of a somewhat faulty linguistic interpretation. Innocent III, in trying to explain the statement in John's gospel (1:42), declared that *cephas* meant *caput*, obviously confusing the Aramaic term *kephas* with the Greek *kephale*. See his *Sermo* II (*Patr. Lat.* ccxvii. 658ª); *Sermo* XVIII (395ᵇ): " 'Tu vocaberis, inquit, Cephas,' quod exponitur *caput*. Utique caput *a capite*, sicut Petrus *a petra*"; *Sermo* VII (482ᶜ); No. XIII (517ᵇ). In No. XXI (552ᶜ), however, he realized that there was some difficulty: "Cephas enim licet secundum unam linguam interpretatur *Petrus* [which in fact was what the John passage said], secundum aliam tamen dicitur *caput*." This linguistic curiosity was already contained in Pseudo-Isidore. See Anacletus in Paul Hinschius, *Decretales Pseudo-Isidorianae* (Berlin, repr. 1960), cap. 33, p. 83. For the royal field which operated on essentially similar premises, see the seventh-century Visigothic laws (*Monumenta Germaniae historica* [hereafter cited as M.G.H.], *Leges Visigothorum* ii. 1. 4), according to which the king was the head and the

Most, if not all, of the basic principles relative to the individual as a subject to higher authority are contained in the Bible, notably in the Pauline letters. If one realizes—as every medievalist ought to, but so few in fact do—what an unparalleled influence the Bible as the repository of divine wisdom exercised in the Middle Ages,[9] one will have no difficulty in appreciating that it was taken not merely as a model, but above all as a ready-made philosophy relative to matters of public government. The all-pervasive Christian theme made the Bible a pattern—a whole philosophy was so conveniently assembled within two covers. Where else could man look for a pattern? Quite especially it is in the Pauline arsenal that the crucial concepts and terms of the subject, of the *subditus,* and the corollary of the higher, of the *sublimis,* as well as the corresponding concept of obedience, appear most fully. One or two examples should illustrate the essential meaning of Pauline expressions. In the letter to the Romans Paul says that because whatever power there is comes from God, every soul should be *subjected* to the higher authorities,[10] from which follows that it is a necessity for the sake of good functioning of the body that individual Christians should be *subjects* of princely power.[11] Titus was advised to bring home to his people the knowledge that they were subjects of the princes and powers and that they therefore had the duty of obedience.[12] The same correla-

---

people the members of the body. The same theme also occurred, of course, in the medieval coronation orders; see, for example, the prayer text on the occasion of conferring the ring (the king as "caput regni et populi").

[9] For some observations see Walter Ullmann, "The Bible and Principles of medieval government," *Settimana di studio di Spoleto,* X (1963), 182ff.; *Studies in Church History,* II (1965), 78ff.; *History of Political Thought in the Middle Ages* (London, 1965), pp. 21f., 52f.

[10] Rom. 13:1–2: "Omnis anima *sublimioribus* potestatibus *subdita* sit."

[11] *Ibid.,* vs.5: "Ideo necessitate *subditi* estote . . ."

[12] Titus 3:1: "Admone illos principibus et potestatibus *subditos* esse, dicto *obedire.*" For the nomocratic conceptions in Paul, see Irene Beck, "Altes und Neues Gesetz," *Münchener Theologische Zeitschrift,* XV (1964), 127ff., esp. 140ff.

tion between subjection and obedience is struck up in another Pauline letter,[13] and exactly the same principle emerged also in one of the Petrine letters.[14] When one realizes that these were not just passages which were read only on specific occasions in the Middle Ages, but that they were statements making basic pronouncements, with which all literate persons in the Middle Ages and especially those who composed the chanceries of the ruling personnel, were familiar, one will perhaps appreciate how much the medieval mind became attuned to these programmatic declarations.

The essential point here is that profound Pauline and deeply Christian themes were in theory and fact transferred to society itself.[15] It was precisely in explaining Pauline doctrine that at the turn of the fourth and fifth centuries John Chrysostom declared that

> . . . it is the divine wisdom and not mere fortuity which has ordained that there should be rulership, that some should order and others should obey.[16]

Nor does it need much historical imagination to visualize the far-reaching effect of yet another Pauline statement: "What I am, I am by the grace of God."[17] In other words, the translation of this latter Pauline thesis was held to entail that the *fidelis christianus* not only had no rights but also had no autonomous standing within the Church itself or within society. Furthermore, the Church itself was always defined as the *congregatio fidelium* or the *universitas fidelium*, in which the accent lay on the *fidelis*. This congregation of the faithful, all-embracing as it was, included both laity

---

[13] Heb. 13:17: "*Obedite* prepositis vestris et *subjacete* eis"; see also I Tim. 2:1-2: Prayers, thanksgiving, and intercessions were to be made "pro regibus et *omnibus* qui in *sublimitate* sunt."

[14] I Pet. 2:13-14.

[15] For the character of the Church as a corporation modeled on Roman law, see above, n. 1.

[16] St. John Chrysostom *In Epistolam ad Romanos* homil. 23 (*Patr. Graeca* lx. 615).

[17] I Cor. 15:10.

and clerics. Indeed, it was the concept of the *fidelis* which
dominated thinking and writing and acting in the medieval
period, because what discerned and distinguished the Christian was his faith. And because he had faith, he obeyed the
law, in the creation of which he had no share. Faith, in other
words, yielded the essential substratum for the validity and
efficacy of the law. Differently expressed, the element of
obedience presupposed the existence of faith. This is indubitably the message of Pauline doctrine. Conceptually it
was impossible to maintain that the *fidelis* could share in
government. We are here presented with an unadulterated
conception of the subject, of the *subditus,* who, by virtue of
his baptism and the consequential incorporation into the
Church, had no autonomous character. Because he had
instead the required faith, he accepted—or perhaps I should
say, was supposed to have accepted—the will of him who
was set above him, the will of the superior.[18] It is this kind
of consideration which makes understandable Augustine's
view that "the Christian is to be led by the weight of
authority" or, conversely, that obedience to the command
of the superior authority was his hallmark.[19]

The concept of the superior and the inferior, the one
above, the other under, seems to me to sum up the function
and status of the individual, at least within the pure
descending doctrine, for only by identifying himself with
the law and government of the superior, that is, by active

[18] That these views on the faithful as a subject are still those of the
modern canon law (see also above) is shown by Carlos M. Corral Sal-
vador, "Incorporación a la Iglesia por el bautismo y sus consecuencias
jurídicas," *Revista Espanola de Derecho Canonico,* XIX (1964), 817ff.,
esp. 828ff. ("el bautizado queda constituido indeblemente *subditus
ecclesiae*").

[19] Augustine *Sermo* CCCLXI 3 (*Patr. Lat.* xxxix. 1600): "Auctoritatis
enim pondere christianus ducendus est"; Augustine *Enarratio in Psalmum*
LXXI (*Patr. Lat.* xxxvi. 904): "[Obedientia] est in hominibus et in omni
rationali creatura omnis justitiae origo atque perfectio"; see also his *De
civitate Dei* xiv. 12, where obedience is called "the mother and guardian
of all virtues."

obedience, could the faithful be and remain one. When, therefore, in the late sixth century Gregory the Great stated that the verdict of the superior—no matter whether just or unjust—had to be obeyed by the inferior subject, he expressed in unmistakable language (which was to be repeated a hundred times throughout the subsequent period) the essential point of the inferior's duty of obedience to the law of the superior.[20]

It was these conceptions of the inferior status of the individual and the superior status of ruling authority which explains not only the prevailing medieval view on the inequality of men—a point to which I will revert in a moment —but also the development of the concept of *majoritas* and its corollary of *obedientia*. Superiority of public rank necessarily yielded the demand for obedience on the part of the inferior subject. To my mind it is, therefore, highly significant that in the fully matured medieval canon law there is a section which bears the very title of *De majoritate et obedientia*. It was in this section of the canon law that the basic legal rules relative to the superior or major authority and the inferior subject were stated, and it was also here that the concept of obedience emerged as an operational concept correlative to major (= superior) authority. Perhaps nothing is more illustrative of this fundamental medieval topic than the postulate for obedience on the part of the subject to the command or law of a superior, although the subject, precisely because he was an inferior,[21] had no share in the making of the command or law, obedience to which was based upon his faith as a Christian. By replacing consent, faith served as the basic ingredient of the law.

That on this ideological basis there resulted a hierarchical ordering of all members of society cannot cause much sur-

---

[20] To the passages cited in Ullmann, *Principles of Government*, p. 107, n. 1, should be added Gratian, xi. 3. 1, and D.a.c.78, *ibid.*

[21] See, for example, the *glossa ordinaria* on *Extravagantes* iii. Ne sede vac., c. un.: "Lex superiori per inferiorem imponi non potest."

prise. This hierarchical ranking was clearly foreshadowed
in Pauline doctrine[22] and was made a special programmatic
point in the late fifth century by Pseudo-Denys,[23] who in
fact coined the very term *hierarchy*. One aspect of this hierarchical thesis was the inequality of the members of society.
One should never forget that the principle of equality is of
fairly recent date; in other words, that the members of
society had, by virtue of being members of society, equality
of standing within the public field was not a doctrine that
was known to the high Middle Ages. Here operated inequality before the law.[24] It is interesting to see how, for
instance, Gregory the Great argued to justify this principle
of inequality. Although nature had made all men equal,
Gregory declared, there nevertheless intervened what he
called "an occult dispensation," according to which some were
set over others "because of the diversity of merits" of the
individuals. He had no doubt that this was in reality the
effluence of the divine ordering of things.[25] The significance
of this basic point of view lay in once again setting aside
what nature had produced—for by nature we are all equals,
he had said—and in replacing the natural ordering by a
purely speculative theorem which in its eventual roots went
back to the fall of man. Again, it is worthy of remark that
this was not merely a doctrinal standpoint, but one that had
concrete applications in the social and public field. Augustine

[22] See Eph. 5:22–24.

[23] See Ullmann, *Principles of Government*, pp. 46f.; *History of Political Thought*, p. 31.

[24] For the similar view of the modern Church, see August Hagen,
Prinzipien des katholischen Kirchenrechts (Würzburg, 1949), p. 178
(the Church had never acknowledged equality of all men or of all
Christians before its forum: if it had done so, it would have denied its
own being); Hugo Schmieden, *Recht und Staat in den Verlautbarungen
der katholischen Kirche seit 1878*, (2d ed.; Bonn, 1961), p. 122.

[25] Gregory I *Moralia* xxi. 15. 22 (*Patr. Lat.* lxxvi. 203): "Omnes
namque homines natura aequales sumus . . . omnes homines natura
aequales genuit, sed variante meritorum ordine, alios aliis dispensatio
occulta postponit. Ipsa autem diversitas, quae accessit ex vitio, recte est
divinis judiciis ordinata."

had already more than hinted at this unequal standing of
the various members of society when he said that it should
be everyman's rule of conduct not to offend a superior,[26] a
point of view which in varying degrees was repeated.[27] The
significance of this hierarchical ranking lay in that through
subordination to the superior there was to come about
an integration of the whole society, thus creating harmony
and order where diversity otherwise would have resulted.
Una concordia ex diversitate (Humbert of Silva Candida)
expressed this idea well enough. The fundamental presupposition, however, was that the individual accepted his standing in society, that he divested himself of his individuality
and will by following the direction "from above," that he, in
other words, obeyed.

The inequality of the members of society showed itself
most manifestly in the unequal treatment before the law,
for a superior was treated differently from an inferior. Once
again Gregory the Great gave the lead when he stated that
those in a commanding position were to be treated differently from those who were subjects.[28] This statement came
to be a major principle: no inferior could legitimately bring
any accusations against a superior. In other words, subjects
were not entitled to invoke the help of a law court against
a superior. From the mid-ninth century this point of view
became universally accepted and had specific reference
within the ecclesiastical sphere and also general reference
within the royal field.[29] Within the former the practical

[26] Augustine *Sermo* LXII 5 (in *Patr. Lat.* xxxviii. 418): "Majorem
certe noli offendere. Haec tibi regula proponitur."
[27] See, for instance, Gregory I *Moralia* xxv. 16. 36 (*Patr. Lat.* lxxvi.
344d): "Quia rectores habent judicem suum, magna cautela subditorum
est non temere vitam judicare regentium."
[28] Gregory I *Regula pastoralis* iii. 4.
[29] See, for example, the Council of Frankfurt presided over by Charlemagne (794), which incorporated the old ruling of the Council of
Carthage, (Jean Dominique Mansi, *Sacrorum Conciliorum Collectio*
[Venice, 1798], III, cap. 8, 714): those who had been convicted of a
crime must not prefer charges against "majores natu aut episcopos suos"
(*M.G.H., Concilia* ii. 170, 36).

consequence was, since the inferior could not judge the superior,[30] that the layman was not only precluded from partaking in matters of ecclesiastical government but also from charging a cleric with any crime, because he was a mere subject.[31] It was merely an extension of this selfsame principle of inequality that inferiors could not make laws by which the superiors could be bound.[32] Perhaps the best illustration of social and legal inequality came in the early seventh century from Isidore of Seville, who combined with it the duty of obedience on the part of the subjects:

> *Superiori aequalem* te non exhibeas. *Senioribus* praesta obedientiam, famulare imperiis eorum, eorum auctoritati cede, obsequere voluntati. Defer obsequia justa majoribus . . .*[33]

Considering that politological thought was so markedly clerical in the earlier and high Middle Ages, one will not be surprised to learn that within the public sphere, the layman as such had none of the rights with which even the most insignificant member of a modern society is credited. He had, for example, no right of resistance to superior authority. Behind all declarations stood the concept of the office, which made possible the distinction between the superior and the inferior, since the office itself was capable of fairly precise measurements. The very nature of hierarchy presupposes a gradation of ranks or offices, according to easily recognizable criteria. It is this feature which imparts practicability to the

[30] See the pseudo-Isidorian passages in Gratian, ii. 7. 4.

[31] The numerous councils of the ninth century made this perfectly clear when they spoke of the "subditi" of priests and bishops, and Pseudo-Isidore in the mid-ninth century frequently stated the same principle. See the passages in Gratian, ii. 7. 1ff. Pope Nicholas I, also in the ninth century, rendered the same principle: *Ep.* 88, in *M.G.H.*, *Epistolae* vi. 469.

[32] See above n. 21; further, see *Liber Extra* i. 33. 16: "Cum inferior *superiorem* solvere nequeat vel ligare, sed superior inferiorem liget regulariter et absolvat . . ."; also see cap. 6, 9, et cetera.

[33] Isidore *Synonyma* ii. 74 (*Patr. Lat.* lxxxiii. 862); similarly, in the twelfth century, Hugh of St. Victor, *Expositio in hierarchiam celestem S. Dionysii* I. 5 (*Patr. Lat.* clxxv. 931).

descending theme of government and explains why those members of society who had no office not only stood at the very bottom of the social ladder but also were without public rights. The individual's standing within society was based upon his office or his official function: the greater it was, the more scope it had, the weightier it was, the more rights the individual had. As a mere subject the individual was no more than a recipient of orders, of commands, of the law, and as a layman, in particular, he was merely a passive spectator who was to obey: his role was that of a learner.[34]

For illustrative purposes permit me to adduce some source material from the high Middle Ages which, although of primary importance to the diplomatist, should be of interest to the historians of governmental ideas as well. The books of instructions for the chancery personnel in the public chanceries contained quite detailed regulations concerning the very points which I have just tried to make.[35] They laid down that a *persona minor* was he who had no public office, such as a merchant, a simple citizen, an artisan, or a person of similar standing.[36] Certain members of society were not even permitted to write or to receive letters to which the ordinary formal requirements were applicable: such persons "who had neither name nor honour" were the lame, the

[34] See, for instance, already the spurious *Epistola Clementis* (composed about the end of the second century), which clearly struck up the theme when it said: "Discentes, id est, laici": *Die Pseudo-Klementinen,* ed. Bernhard Rehm in *Die griechischen christlichen Schriftsteller* (Berlin, 1953), 5. 4. 9. ll. 28–29. This principle of functions within society was a point in the genuine epistle of Clement I sent to the Corinthians: it was in this letter that the term *laikos* appeared for the first time; see Ullmann, *Principles of Government,* p. 67, n. 1.

[35] About the great importance of these so-called diplomatic formulae, see Walter Ullmann in *Annali della Fondazione Italiana per la Storia Amministrativa,* I (1964), 117ff.

[36] See, for example, Ludolf, *Summa dictaminum,* or the Formulary of Baumgartenberg, both of the thirteenth century, in Ludwig Rockinger, *Briefsteller und Formelbücher* (Munich, 1863), pp. 361f. and 727: minor persons are "mercatores, cives simplices, et artis mechanicae professores et omnes consimiles carentes dignitatibus."

blind, and the like.[37] The general rule was that when a superior wrote to an inferior subject, certain terms of an imperative character had to be employed; vice versa, the inferior subject writing to the superior had to use "adverbia *subjectionis.*"[38] These chancery books allow the discerning student unimpeded ingress into the workshop of the governments themselves and deserve, along with similar source material, greater attention than they have hitherto received.

It would be quite misleading and erroneous to think that my foregoing considerations apply only to the ecclesiological set of ideas, for, as I have already had occasion to remark, it was no different in the royal field proper, where it was very much the same premise by which the individual was absorbed in the body corporate of the kingdom. If anything, the individual was far less in a position to assert any autonomous rights, because the possibility of a distinction between private and public, which was to some extent operative in the ecclesiastical field, was for the greater part of the Middle Ages not drawn in the royal sphere. Here the very concept of subject, of the *subditus,* of the *Untertan,* was in actual fact far more, and more directly, an operational instrument. Often enough do we read in the royal field that the *populus* was *commissus* to the king—that the people or the kingdom was entrusted to the king's government—just as we read in the ecclesiastical domain that the Church was committed to the pope's government. This was not a mere formula nor a device of some high-sounding chancery practice, but a statement with profound contents.

That the kingdom or the people were entrusted or committed to the king's government meant, firstly, that the king's

[37] See Conrad of Mure, *Summa de arte prosandi, ibid.,* p. 429.
[38] See Guido Faba (*ca.* 1230), *ibid.,* p. 186, no. 1: "Si majores, clerici vel layci, prelati ecclesiastici vel domini saeculares, *subditis vel minoribus* scripserint, materiam per ista verba poteris incipere preceptiva: mandamus, precipimus, instantissime, constanter, indubitanter, et peremptorie"; p. 188, no. 3: "Principia de subditis et minoribus"; p. 197: "De episcopis ad subditos"; and so on.

power itself was not derived from the people or the kingdom or any individuals, but from divinity. The title of the king as "King by the grace of God" expressed the idea that his powers were the result of the working of God's good will or of God's grace, which was merely another way of applying the Pauline thesis that what I am, I am by the grace of God,[39] or seen from another angle, that the kingdom or the people or the totality of the individuals had nothing to do with the powers which the king possessed. The king received his powers as a concession from divinity—another Pauline principle was concretely applied: there is no power but of God—and what he had received through the grace of God in the shape of public power, he could concede to his subjects. The individuals as subjects had no rights in the public field. Whatever they had, they had as a matter of royal grace, of royal concession.[40] One will understand now, I hope, why the king's grace was so vitally important for the subjects, for without it they had no standing in public: this is the vital contrast of the king's grace and his disgrace, the latter of which the subject incurred if for the one or the other reason he had jeopardized the king's good will

[39] See above, n. 17. Thus, Count Boso of Burgundy designated himself in exactly this way in a document dated July 25, 879: "Ego Boso, Dei gratia id quod sum." See F. Dümmler, *Geschichte des ostfränkischen Reiches,* (2d ed.; Leipzig, 1888), p. 132.

[40] It should by no means be assumed that this kind of argumentation was characteristic of the medieval period only. On the very eve of the American Revolution, statements were made by the defenders of the *status quo* which, though anachronistic at the time, nevertheless betray a proper medieval spirit. Thus Jonathan Boucher declared in 1775 that "kings and princes . . . were doubtless created and appointed not so much for their own sakes as for the sake of the people committed to their charge; yet they are not, therefore, the creatures of the people. So far from deriving their authority from any supposed consent or suffrage of men, they receive their commission from Heaven; they receive it from God, the source and origin of all power. . . ." And to him the duty of the subjects is, in the phraseology of a prophet, "to be quiet and to sit still"; quoted in Bernard Baylin, (ed.), *Pamphlets of the American Revolution 1750-1776* (Cambridge, Mass., 1965), I, 201. See also *ibid.,* p. 197, for Isaac Hunt's similar anachronistic view, also of 1775, of the principle of subordination and obedience to the superior.

and caused his *benevolentia* to turn into *malevolentia*. And this is the deeper meaning of the medieval penalty of the amercement—the subject had lost the mercy, the good will of the king, and in order to regain it, had to pay a fine or some other compensation. One has but to read through the thousands of medieval charters and diplomata to realize how potently this ideology was entrenched, so entrenched, in fact, that to this day in England one can daily read in the official *London Gazette* that the queen has "graciously appointed" an individual to a particular post or has "graciously conferred" the office of Governor General or the office of High Commissioner or has "graciously approved" of the appointments made by the Prime Minister, and so on. These expressions portray distinctly the idea of royal grace and employ language which very clearly links the present age with the early Middle Ages. What this medieval thesis of royal grace (or its counterpart, royal disgrace) meant was stated in graphic manner at a time when it had no longer any practical meaning. A statement of James I which could have been made in the high Middle Ages, leaves nothing to be desired by way of clarity:

> The plain truth is [he said] that we cannot with patience endure our subjects to use such anti-monarchic words to us, concerning their liberties, except that they had subjoined that they were granted unto them by grace and favour of our predecessors.

The essential point of the concession thesis is that whatever rights a subject has, he has as the effluence of the king's good will, of the king's own grace, which was a favor and which the subjects could not claim as a right. One has no right to claim a good deed, to claim a favor.

In addition to the people's (the aggregate of all the individuals) or the kingdom's being in the trust of the king, there is, secondly, the thesis that the individuals as members of the people were in the *Munt* of the king. Now this was a

crucial governmental concept in all medieval kingdoms and
also one of the oldest concepts which clearly indicated that
the individual as well as the people had no autonomous
power. The *Munt* (Latin: *Mundium* or *mundeburdium;*
Anglo-Saxon: *mundbora;* old-French: *mainbour;* Italian:
Manovaldo [= mundoaldus])[41] placed people on the same
level as a minor under age and meant the supreme protection, the over-all superior and controlling knowledge of the
king of when and how and where and why the subjects
needed his protection. One can best understand the meaning
of the *Munt* if one compares it to the guardianship of a
child: it is the kind of protection which a father affords to
a child, or a guardian to his ward, or in Anglo-Saxon and
Anglo-Norman England the husband to his wife.[42] The
kingdom or the people in the trust of the king were treated—

[41] For the late Roman conditions see Cassiodore *Varia* ii. 29; vii. 39;
etc. For modern literature see Adolf Waas, *Herrschaft und Staat im
deutschen Frühmittelalter* (Tübingen, 1938); Walter Schlesinger in
Historische Zeitschrift, CLXXVI (1953), 237ff.; Ullmann, *Principles of
Government,* pp. 126f. All the expressions mentioned in the text probably
go back to *manus.* In modern German there are still *Vor/mund, Mündel,
Ent/mündigung; mündig;* etc. One of the earliest royal applications of
the concept of the *Munt* I have found is that by King Childeberth I in
the year 528; he gave a number of privileges to monks and said this:
"Per hanc auctoritatem a nobis firmatam sub immunitatis nostrae tuitione
vel *mundeburdie* quietos residere"; M.G.H., *Diplomata regum Francorum*
5.2.

[42] In Anglo-Saxon England marriage was constituted by the sale of the
Munt, which the bridegroom bought from the bride's parents or guard-
ians: she then came under the *Munt* of her husband, who controlled her
and whom she had to obey. What is also interesting is that the wife could
not in Anglo-Norman England transact any legal business without the
husband's permission; see *Leges Henrici Primi* (ca. 1114–18) 45. 3 (in
F. Liebermann, *Die Gesetze der Angelsachsen,* II [Halle, 1913], 570),
where she was put on the same level as a boy or a girl and where the
husband was called her *dominus.* See also below for the consequences of
her murdering the husband. For further details concerning husband and
wife, see Frederick Pollock and Frederic William Maitland, *History of
English Law* (2d ed.; Cambridge, 1926), II, 403ff., esp. 406, where
Maitland speaks of an "exaggerated guardianship" by the husband; here
also quotations from Glanvill, et cetera. We should bear in mind that
many of the reasons for the wife's subjection to her husband were derived
from Paul's view that the husband was "the head of the wife."

and explicitly so—as if they had been minors who needed the protecting and guiding hand of the king.

There may well have been adequate and justifiable reasons for this view, and we should not measure this fundamental conception by modern standards. It is not necessary to exercise one's historical imagination to realize how little knowledge of the matters which were the concern of governments could in fact be presupposed not only among the rural population but also among the townsfolk. In obvious contrast to modern conditions, the individual as a subject had no means to inform himself; he had not much opportunity of acquainting himself with any of the issues at stake, and he could not be expected to have an adequate grasp of the matters which the king, by virtue of his own governmental apparatus, necessarily possessed. It is against this sort of background that one can understand not only the preponderant influence of Platonic and Neo-Platonic ideas in the Middle Ages[43] but also the requirement postulated in all spheres of theocratic governments—whether papal, royal, or imperial makes no difference—the requirement of knowledge, of *scientia*, with which the subjects, precisely because they were subjects, were not credited. One can also understand the allegorical utilization of the head to symbolize the *potestas regitiva*, or in a roundabout way one can here apply the concept of office, because its hallmark was special knowledge (*scientia*) and a special power (*potestas*), both evidently relative to the kind of office which the individual occupied.[44]

At the same time we should not think that the subjects in any way felt that they were oppressed or suppressed. The

[43] See Endre von Ivánka, *Plato Christianus* (Einsiedeln, 1964), especially pp. 309ff., also 476f.

[44] Indeed, Hegel's view on Platonism that its essential feature was the suppression of individuality appears to be supported by the medieval application of Platonic axioms, powerfully advocated as they had been by Augustine, who called Plato the most Christian of pagan philosophers.

awareness of being suppressed presupposes considerable knowledge and critical judgment. Furthermore, the individuals and their aggregate, the people, had every opportunity of expressing their requests, petitions, and aims; and in times of stress and tension the king was well advised to listen to the people, but—and this is the crucial point—a right to demand action or a duty on the part of the king to carry out the petitions of the people could by no means be constructed or was even asserted. This is a point which we should do well to keep in mind if we wish to assess the importance and the fructifying effects of the feudal system. The ideology concerning royal power in the Middle Ages showed—in no wise differently from the ecclesiastical thesis —that the individual was placed *under* the tutelage of those who had been selected by divinity[15] as the trustees of the people, of those to whom the people or the kingdom (or for that matter the Church) was entrusted.[46]

An immediate, practical as well as theoretical consequence of this ideology was the king's duty to care for his subjects, a duty which was in fact embodied in the concept of the *Munt*. This duty was always made a strong point in all

[45] Apart from Old Testament models, there were numerous early Christian testimonies which made this a specific point. See, for instance, Origines *Homilia* 22. ad Num. c. 27: "Gubernatio populi illi tradatur quem Deus elegerit, homini scilicet tali, qui habet, sicut scriptum audistis, in semetipso spiritum Dei et precepta Dei" (incorporated in Gratian and ascribed to Jerome in viii. 1. 16); Justinian in his *Novella* viii. Epilogue: "Traditae nobis a Deo reipublicae curam habentes"; hence, his constant preoccupation with rendering justice to his subjects (*ibid.*, Preface, and cap. 11); *Novella* iv. Epilogue ("cautela *subjectorum*"); *Novella* lxxiii. Preface (giving the law "in commune *subjectis*"); *Novella* cxxx. Epilogue; *Novella* cxxxiv. Preface ("ad utilitatem *nostrorum subjectorum*" was the law issued); et cetera. See, further, Council of IV Toledo (in Mansi, *Concil. Coll.*, x, 640); Smaragdus, *Via regia* (*Patr. Lat.* cii. 933ᵇ): "Constituit te [Dominus] regem populi terrae, et proprii Filii sui in coelo fieri jussit *haeredem*"; and so forth.

[46] See, also, for example, some of the statements made by councils in the ninth century: e.g., Council of Arles (813): "populus commissus imperatori" (Charlemagne) (*M.G.H., Concilia* i. 248. l. 25); Council of Paris (829): "populus sibi (imperatori) *subjectus*" (*ibid.*, 612. 5); Council of Aachen (836): "populus vobis *subjectus*" (*ibis.*, 767.27); et cetera.

doctrinal expositions on kingship, including the numerous
Specula regum, and what is particularly interesting is that
in this specific instance one notices a confluence of old
Germanic and Pauline views, for the Pauline advice was
frequently invoked to show the biblical foundation of this
duty.[47] The concept of kingship was held to contain the
obligation toward the so-called feebler members, to use this
Pauline expression. But no right on the part of the subjects
corresponded to this royal duty: they had nothing to do with
the office of kingship, which was an emanation of the divine
good will toward the king. The king's position in regard to
his subjects was envisaged on a level similar to that of a
father to his family. Numerous testimonies there are which
urged the king to manage his government in a manner
profitable to his subjects. These statements were, however,
merely of an exhortatory character.[48] This duty was also
expressed in no less formal a place than in the Arengae of
royal or imperial documents. Thus, for instance, Charles III
in 887 stated in a diploma that it behoved imperial dignity
"curam *omnium subjectorum* gerere,"[49] and most interestingly, the subjects were in the same place designated as
"cuncti fideles."[50] In the manner of classical Roman writers,
notably Cicero, the ruler was often enough said to be "the
common father of all" ("communis pater omnium"), and the

[47] See I Cor. 12:22.
[48] See, for instance, Isidore of Seville *Synonyma* ii. 77 (*Patr. Lat.*
lxxxiii. 862): "Summa bonitate subditos rege, non sis terribilis in subjectis"; Isidore *Sententiae* iii. 49 (*ibid.,* 721ᵃ): "Dedit Deus principibus praesulatum pro regimine populorum, illis eos praeesse voluit . . . nec
dominando premere, sed condescendo consulere . . ."; *ibid.,* 48 (*ibid.,*
718ᵇ–19ᵇ): "Tunc autem bene geritur [scil. insigne potestatis], quando
subjectis prodest . . . Recte enim illi reges vocantur, qui tam semetipsos
quam subjectos, bene regendo modificare noverunt." See also Gregory I
(incorporated in Gratian, xi. 3. 61): "Judicare de subditis digne
nequeunt qui in subditorum causa sua vel odia vel gratiam sequuntur."
[49] *M.G.H., Diplomata* ii: DK III. 166. 269.
[50] ". . . idcirco cunctorum fidelium." This identification of the subjects
with the faithful was quite common at the time. See, e.g., Council of
Cabillon (813), in *M.G.H., Concilia* i. 9 and 10. p. 276; of Paris (825),
ibid., 483. 42; Paris (829), *ibid.,* 616. 9; et cetera.

deduction drawn from this was that the ruler's government of his subjects was similar to the relation of a father to his children, of the pastor to his flock, for "in a fatherly manner he should govern his people."[51] In fact, there was virtually no commentary or tract that did not in one way or another emphasize this royal duty; yet, it was a purely one-sided obligation which the subjects had no means of enforcing in a legal manner, which they could not demand because they had no rights. True enough, it was often stated—and sometimes quite forcefully, for instance, by John of Salisbury[52]— that "the feebler members" were necessary for the smooth operation and function of the public body, but this recognition was a very long way from ascribing to the subjects (such as the feebler members indubitably were) any indigenous, autonomous rights with which they could confront the king. If he did not fulfill this duty of his, no power existed on earth to make him do it. The frequency of these hortatory statements stood in inverse proportion to the practical as well as theoretical feasibility of translating them into reality.

Another practical consequence of this subjection of the individual to the superior concerned the right of resistance: within the cluster of theocratic ideas it would have been very hard to construct any such right, for the question arose at once as to how to prove this right of resistance. Where did the individual as a mere subject get this right? Not only was the well-known Pauline thesis of not offering resistance to ordained power readily at hand, for to resist power was to resist divine ordinance, but there was also the consideration that the king was the Lord's anointed, the *christus domini*,[53] who by virtue of the unction had been shown in a most

[51] Lucas de Penna: "Similis est *operatio regis ad subjectos* patris ad filios, pastoris ad oves: *paterno* enim *more* pie debet regere populum"; cited by Walter Ullmann, *The Medieval Idea of Law* (London, 1946), p. 186, n. 5.

[52] See Ullmann, *Principles of Government*, p. 230.

[53] The idea and expression were biblical. See I Paral. 16: 22; I Reg. 26: 11, 16, 23; et cetera.

tangible and visible way to be the recipient of God's favor—
unction was the one concrete element which lifted the king
out of the mass of all his subjects, because unction was the
means by which God's grace was *seen* to have entered the
king's body. How could a *right* of resistance be asserted
against him whom divinity had selected in so palpable a
manner? I am sure that there is no need to refer specifically
to the very real difficulties presented by a king whose government had become tyrannical. The only road open was either
to commit regicide—which is not really a constitutional step
—or to pray for the king's conversion, which too does not
seem to fall within the constitution. The fact that both suggestions were made by eminent writers clearly indicates how
difficult it was to deal with the king by the grace of God who
had turned out to be a tyrant.

The king's having had God's authority—hence also his
having been designated as God's vicegerent on earth or
God's vicar—in theory and largely also in practice removed
him from the control of the very men for whose guidance
and care he was established in the first place; the king as the
Lord's anointed could not be withstood or resisted or subjected to any control by those over whom divinity had set
him.[54] Indeed, since Paul himself had made the ruler a
"minister Dei"[55] and since he also considered everybody
subjected to higher power, it would have been nothing less
than rebellion against divinity, itself meriting eternal punishment, for the subject to resist the king.[56] But quite apart
from this, what individual or what body or group was by
law entitled to declare the king's government tyrannical?
Who was qualified to pronounce that the Lord's anointed
oppressed his subjects? This problem was as insoluble as the

[54] Of course Paul was again to be invoked. See Rom. 13: p.t.; Eph. 6:
1ff.; 5: 22–24; et cetera.

[55] Rom. 13: 4.

[56] It was no coincidence that this very same Pauline text was incorporated prominently in the coronation service.

parallel problem in the ecclesiastical field: who was entitled
to declare the pope heretical? If the principle of concession
is taken seriously enough, the insolubility of this problem is
self-evident.

Considering the strongly pronounced superior-inferior relationship between king and subject, it is interesting to see
the consequence of criminal conduct against the king: it was
nothing but *high* treason, and the very term and concept of
high treason is a vivid reminder of the underlying ideology.
Treason was committed against the highness of the king,
against his high status, against his *majestas*,[57] and the very
concept of *majestas* is itself, of course, a very strong pointer
to the prevailing ideology, *majestas* designating the office and
the function of him who was major. This was indeed the
constant doctrine—and probably also practice—in the Middle
Ages.[58] *Majestas* was explained as "quasi major stans," as a
power which stood higher than any other power, and the
crime of treason could not be committed by a mere vassal
of the ruler—which is a highly significant exception—but
solely by a subject.[59] What in actual fact amounted to high

[57] For the meaning of the term *majestas*, which is of Roman origin,
see Georges Dumézil, "Maiestas et gravitas," *Revue de philologie* 3d
ser.; vol. XXVI, 1952, pp. 7ff.; see especially p. 17: "A l'époque
ancienne dans la Rome royale, maiestas était de même la caractéristique
des rois . . . sous la république elle reste des hommes qui sont les plus
près de Jupiter, ou qui 'incarnent' Jupiter, tant les consuls que l'imperator
triomphant. Plus tard elle appartiendra au princeps, pui, à travers lui,
aux rois du moyen âge." Hence, also, the appellation of "Your Highness,"
which is a translation of the medieval *altitudo*, frequently employed; see,
e.g., the Merovingian King Childeric II in 673 ("monasterium . . . petiit
altitudinem nostram") in *M.G.H., Dipl. R. Francorum* 30.31, or Charles
III in 885 ("hoc nostrae *altitudinis* pactum") in *M.G.H., Diplomata
regum et imperatorum Germaniae* ii.122.194.

[58] It may be recalled that the first statutory enactment of any criminal
law in England was made in 1352 by Edward III; see William S. Holdsworth, *History of English Law* (2d ed.; London, 1926), III, 249.

[59] See, for example, Oldradus da Ponte, *Consilia* (Frankfurt, 1568)
Cons. 43. fol. 15vb. no. 8: "Majestas dicitur quasi major stans sive major
potestas, arguendo ergo a ratione nominis . . . *subditus* committens in
principem, committit crimen *laesae majestatis*, sed in non subdito non est
ista lex imposita."

treason evidently depended upon positive law, but the one essential ingredient of the crime was that the action at least be aimed at offending the divine power represented in the king. High treason was clearly seen as something which violated the very core of the king's sublime status; it was, therefore, rather apt to bring the Pauline view on resistance to divine ordinance clearly into full view. It is, moreover, not in the least insignificant that the inferior-superior relationship which so markedly appears in high treason constituted also the reason for declaring "petty treason," murder of the master (the superior) by his servant (the inferior), or murder of the bishop by a clerk or a layman of his diocese, or murder of the husband by the wife.[60]

There is really no need to elaborate on the symbolic meaning of the throne, upon which the king sat visibly elevated and exalted—higher (*major*) than any of those entrusted to him. Even the dullest, most insensitive and illiterate subject of the king became perfectly aware of his own inferior status when he looked up to the *majestas* enthroned. It is also noteworthy that in medieval western Europe the throne came to be the symbol of kingly *majestas* (or his *sublimitas*) at the time when theocratic kingship began its triumphant career, that is, in the eighth century. Furthermore, the symbol had a clearly discernible biblical origin[61] and betrayed also some ancient Roman and Germanic roots.[62] It

[60] This was Anglo-Saxon law, also incorporated in the English statute of 1352. In 1828 these offences were made simple cases of murder; see Holdsworth, *English Law*, II, 373.

[61] See III Reg. 10:9: "[Deus] *posuit* te *super thronum* Israel"; also III *Reg.* 1:35 and 46.

[62] In Rome the *cathedra* or *sella* were symbols of the power of public officers. The former became also the bishop's seat by the third century; see the Muratorian canon in Carl Mirbt, *Quellen zur Geschichte des Papsttums und des römischen Katholizismus* (4th ed.; Tübingen, 1924), no. 31, p. 14, ll. 74ff., and Hans Ulrich Instinsky, *Bischofsstuhl und Kaiserthron* (Munich, 1955); and for the Germanic pattern, see Percy Ernst Schramm, *Herrschaftszeichen und Staatssymbolik* (in *Schriften der M.G.H.* [Stuttgart, 1956ff.], I, 316ff., 336ff.)

is, therefore, easily understandable that the coronation services devoted special attention to the king's enthronement
and the accompanying solemn and pregnant prayer texts.
These texts and the benedictions belong to the oldest stock
of the coronation ritual, and they leave no doubt about the
meaning of the throne as a visible means to present the king
as "high" above the people, occupying, symbolically, an
estate of his own which because of its sublimity cannot be
shared by anybody else. The rubric heading the ancient and
sonorous prayer text *Sta et retine* indeed means what it says:
it is the *designatio status regii*. Through enthronement the
king assumed the royal status by occupying a seat high above
his subjects in his kingdom. The superior-inferior relationship could hardly be better presented. Appropriately the
enthronement was always the last ceremonial action in any
royal coronation proceedings—the other acts, such as the
coronation itself, the conferment of the individual symbols
(scepter, rod, armils, ring, et cetera) were preparatory to his
occupying the throne. Not without reason, therefore, did
the directions of the coronation proceedings lay special stress
on the preparation of "the high throne" (*thronus excelsus*),
so that "the king may be clearly beholden by the people."

What is of further interest in this context is that, at any
rate, the German medieval kings had not only in their palatine
residences thrones, on which they sat during official functions,
but also so-called traveling folding stools (*faldistoria*) for the
occasions on which they had to camp in the open or had
to reside in another castle.[63] In other words, the sublime
status of the king, his majesty, had to be brought to the
attention of the subjects on all conceivable occasions. In
passing, it should be noted that between the folding stools
of the kings and those used by bishops for similar purposes
there was no difference.[64] It was while sitting on the throne

[63] See Percy Ernst Schramm, *Denkmale der deutschen Könige und
Kaiser* (Munich, 1962), p. 36.
[64] See *ibid.*, col. 2, for examples.

that the king received the supplications of his subjects, received homage, and acted in a royal capacity.[65] Once again, a highly developed symbolism served to bring into clearest possible relief the abstract relationship between the inferior and the superior.

One could hardly expect that these ideological premises would facilitate constitutional progress. If the subjects were mere recipients of the law given them, and if the law was, as was often enough said and written and stated, a gift of God, a *donum Dei*, made known through the mouth of the king, how could progress be made in a constitutional respect and the subject released from the fetters into which this doctrine had put him? Any incipient opposition at once smacked of sacrilege since these basic conceptions were of a theocentric, Pauline pedigree. One has only to look at and analyse properly such notions and terms as *dignitas, honor, gratia, beneficium, salus,* and so on, with which official, semi-official, and literary writings teem to realize their theocentric background. These were not just bombastic or sanctimonious or naïve terms, but concepts which had translated—or perhaps I should say, had attempted to translate—the profound Pauline doctrine into mundane matters of government: nobody has a right to demand an honor, nobody is entitled to claim a good deed, and so on.[66] What all forms of theocratic government made abundantly clear was that man was to be subjected to a power which was outside and above man himself, superior to him, a power over which he had no control.

In particular, what characterized all forms of the descend-

[65] For the throne symbolism in Constantinople, where the idea of the *majestas* was still more developed than in the West, see Otto Treitinger, *Die oströmische Kaiser-und Reichsidee* (2d ed.; Darmstadt, 1956), pp. 32ff., 199ff.

[66] The individual's prayers—to which the divine (or royal) conferment of *gratia, dignitas,* et cetera, was held to have been the answer—were by their very nature mere supplications, containing no shade of any assertion of a right on the part of the individual.

ing theme of government and law in the Middle Ages was that the ancient requirement of the consent of the citizen was replaced by the faith of the subjects, for it was the faith in the substance of Christianity which gave birth to the theocratic institutions themselves. Moreover, the king within the descending theme of government did not belong to the kingdom; the pope did not belong, in his function as pope, to the Church—each stood outside and above the entity entrusted to him. To "No writ runs against the king" and "Princeps legibus solutus" corresponded "Papa a nemine judicatur," and all these maxims expressed the same thing: no subject could call the ruler to account.[67] The ruler formed an estate of his own; he formed a corporation sole, established and ordained as he was by divinity for the sake of governing and guiding the people, as the prayer texts of the numerous coronation services amply and incontrovertibly prove. And the corollary on the individual's side was obedience to the ruler's laws, emanating as they did from a divinely instituted superior. Understanding of the nature of superior and inferior roles should not lead, however, to the assumption that the will of the ruler was, so to speak, imposed, as a conqueror imposes his will upon a conquered population. Rather the construction chosen in the Middle Ages was that obedience was simply the outward sign of faith and that the ruler demanded from his subjects nothing that was not already contained in the unquestioned and unrestricted faith of the subjects. Since faith was all-embracing, compliance with the law given by the superior followed as a matter of course. The whole complex theme of *obedientia facit imperantem* resolves itself in the Middle Ages into a co-operating accept-

[67] The jurists in the medieval universities also operated with, and elaborated the Roman law dicta of, "Omnia jura princeps habet in suo pectore" (The prince has all the laws in his breast) or "Quod principi placuit, habet legis vigorem" (What pleases the prince has the force of law). The modern canon law of the Roman Church still has the maxim quoted in the text.

ance by the inferior subject of the superior's decrees and laws, because the subject has faith in the superior's institution. The eulogies which the virtue of obedience received in the Middle Ages[68] are, therefore, easily understandable, for obedience was the external sign of faith in the institution, was the yardstick which offered a ready measurement for the degree of the individual's subjection.[69] That these postulates were intimately linked with the medieval search for unity seems so evident that no comment is called for.

The absorption of the individual by the community or by society accounts for a number of features with which every medievalist is familiar. There is no need here to refer to collective punishments, such as the interdict of a locality or the amercements of towns, villages, or hundreds, and so on: the basic view seems to have been the corporate character of the group, and it made not the slightest difference how many innocent suffered from these impositions.

Moving to an entirely different manifestation of the absorption of the individual by society, that is, the anonymity of writers, scholars, pamphleteers, chancery personnel, architects, scribes, and so on, I can only testify to my own annoyance—though I feel I am not alone in experiencing this reaction—when I come across a work of art or of literature or of documentation which so successfully hides its author. What do we know of the men who conceived and executed some of the finest architectural works still the marvel of even this highly sophisticated generation? Who wrote this or that tract which often started a new line of thought or even a

---

[68] See also above, nn. 19, 20.

[69] See, for instance, Gregory I *Moralia* xxxv., 14. 18 (*Patr. Lat.* lxxvi. 765): "Sola (obedientia) quae *fidei meritum* possidet"; *ibid.*, 14. 28 (*ibid.*, 765b): "Sola namque virtus est obedientia quae virtutes caeteras menti inserit, insertasque custodit. Unde et primus homo praeceptum quod servaret, accepit, cui se si vellet *obediens subdere*, ad aeternam beatitudinem sine labore perveniret . . ."; *ibid.* (*ibid.*, 766a): "Nobis quippe obedientia usque ad mortem servanda praecipitur"; et cetera. These were statements which re-echoed throughout the Middle Ages.

school? As often as not we are confronted with a *siglum* at
the end of a gloss or of a *Summa,* but who was B? Who
was M? There were many Bernards, and there were many
Martins.[70] In the case of official documents this anonymity
is particularly serious: who was the head of the chancery
at this or that time, drafting this or that decree or law with
its beautifully arranged Arenga? To be told that it was
chancery clerk W_1 or B_4 really does not help matters very
much. Who conceived Ely Cathedral? Who was the architect of Strasbourg Cathedral? Who were the builders of the
dozens of magnificent monuments? To be told, again, that
this work comes from the school of Reichenau and that work
from the school of St. Albans, and so on, is really no substi-
tute for an identification of the individual who composed
and executed or illuminated this or that manuscript. Today
when a new apartment house goes up, the name of its
architect is splashed all over the papers, but in coming ages
neither the architect nor his building will be remembered,
while after so many centuries medieval productions still
evoke justifiably great admiration.

Similar observations apply to the lack of individuality in
handwriting. Paleographical examinations are—I speak from
experience—some of the trickiest and most treacherous examinations a medievalist is forced to take. To be sure, one
can distinguish between Italian and Anglo-Norman scrip-
toria, but this does not seem to help very much because there
were hundreds of "graduates" from these schools, and every
one of them exhibited exactly the same traits, the same
scribal features which often spanned a whole century. It is
indeed very hard sometimes to detect any kind of individuality in the handwriting itself, which, I would be inclined

[70] In this context see the observations of Ernst Robert Curtius,
Europäische Literatur und Lateinisches Mittelalter (2d ed.; Berne, 1954),
Excursus XVII, pp. 503–5: it is especially interesting to note that from
the twelfth century on the author's name appeared more and more frequently (p. 505), though juristic writings continued to be anonymous
down to the thirteenth century.

to think, aimed at producing the impersonal character of the modern letterpress.

A symptom which may incontrovertibly indicate how little standing the individual had is the absence of what we nowadays call the majority principle in voting procedures. We are so familiar with it that we do not realize its fairly recent origin. Throughout the greater part of the Middle Ages decisions made by corporate bodies were not arrived at by the operation of the numerical or quantitative majority principle, but by a qualitative majority. This was usually expressed by the *pars sanior* (or similar terms), which did not take into account the exact numbers voting on either side, but the greater weight of those voters who had a higher authority, partly by virtue of their office and partly by virtue of greater knowledge, learning, experience, or the consideration which they derived from their rank. In other words, it was not the individual casting his vote who counted; it was the value which he had to the corporate body; it was his position and function which were reflected in the weight attributed to his vote and which counted. Only when all the voters had the same office, hence the same standing, was the qualitative majority replaced by the quantitative-numerical principle, as could be witnessed in the procedure adopted for papal elections (1179), when a two-thirds majority was required: because no distinction between the voting cardinals could be drawn, counting by heads only remained.[71]

On the other hand, one can hardly doubt that the requirement of the rule of unanimity on certain occasions, such as in the medieval English jury system, was connected with

[71] See Otto Gierke, "Ueber die Geschichte des Majoritätsprinizips," *Schmollers Jahrbuch* (1915), pp. 289ff.; J. G. Heinberg, in *Political Science Review*, XX (1926), 52ff.; L. Moulin, in *Revue historique de droit français et étranger*, XXXVI (1958), 368ff.; J. Gaudement, in *Etudes historiques à la mémoire de Noel Didier* (Paris, 1960), pp. 149ff. The majority principle of the election decree was by some writers also applied to consistorial decisions; see the passages in Brian Tierney, *Foundations of the Conciliar Theory* (Cambridge, 1955), pp. 81–82.

the functions of the jurors, who spoke not for themselves and who issued their *veredictum* (verdict) not as their own, but who spoke "for the country." Here a majority rule, of whatever shape, would have failed to implement what Maitland once called the communal principle, because the parties to a conflict had "put themselves" upon the country, and the verdict of the jurors was the verdict of the country. How could the verdict of the country be divided? "Just as a corporation can have but one will, so a country can have but one voice: *le pays vint e dyt.*"[72] There is some evidence, however, that a simple majority was not unknown to Anglo-Norman England: in the *Leges Henrici Primi* of the second decade of the twelfth century, we read that "if there is dissension amongst the parties in the course of the trial, the majority opinion shall prevail."[73] Significantly, the study of Roman law in the medieval universities had a considerable share in weakening the monopolistic position of the qualitative principle.[74]

[72] Pollock and Maitland, *English Law*, II, 626. Maitland also suggests as a further reason for the unanimity rule (p. 627) that it saved the judges from "that as yet unattempted task, a critical dissection of testimony." This is certainly true, but the very difficulty of assessing the credibility of witnesses presupposes, as every practicing lawyer and judge knows, not only a great deal of analytical perception, but also an appraisal of the witness's personality, his individuality, his bearing, his conduct during the trial, and so on. But the voice of the country (or of the neighborhood), on the one hand, reflects the corporational (Maitland's communal) principle and, on the other hand, dispenses the judiciary from an evaluation of the individual's worth as a witness.

[73] F. Liebermann, *Die Gesetze der Angelsachsen*, I (Halle, 1903), 5.6. p. 549: "Quodsi in judicio inter partes oriatur dissensio, de quibus emerserit certamen, vincat sententia plurimorum." But there was no consistency about it; see *ibid.*, 31.2. p. 564 ("sententia meliorum"), with ed. note (b).

[74] See Dig. 50. 1. 19; Dig. 50. 17. 160(1); Dig. 4. 8. 32; Odofredus, *ibid.*, *et alii*. Odofredus even maintained that if a body had 600 members, and only 400 appeared, 201 members constituted the majority and bound the other 399 members. For a similar view held by Hugolinus, see the passage in Otto Gierke, *Das deutsche Genossenschaftsrecht* (Berlin, 1868–1913), III, 222, n. 110: "Quod universitas vel major pars vel illi qui a majore parte universitatis electi sunt, faciunt, perinde ac si tota universitas faceret." For a similar principle in Magna Carta, see also below, p. 78.

Here some specific observations are called for regarding the medieval thesis of the corporational structure of society, rooted as this was in Roman conceptions. Students of medieval history are familiar with the trite postulate *Utilitas publica prefertur utilitati privatae*. In drawing attention to this medieval maxim, I am well aware of the resuscitation of this very same maxim in more recent days, but we should not forget that a considerable span of time has intervened between the medieval application of the principle and its modern revival. The significance of this principle in the medieval period is that what mattered was the public weal, the public welfare, the public well-being, in brief, the good of society itself, even at the expense of the individual well-being if necessary. If we were to try to pursue the matter a little further, we would understand on the one hand why the law played so crucial a role in the Middle Ages, for law, in order to be law, is at all times addressed to the generality, and on the other hand the very real concern of medieval governments for safeguarding the interests of society, that is, the public good, which was considered to be the *supremum bonum*. From this consideration arose the demand for suppressing publicly all individual opinion contrary to the assumptions upon which society allegedly was built.

The most readily available instance in this respect is the inquisitorial procedure which was based upon the consideration that the cementing bond of the corporate body, that is, the faith, must be safeguarded under all circumstances. Society was one whole and was indivisible, and within it the individual was no more than a part: but what mattered was the well-being of society and not the well-being of the individual parts constituting it. The individual was so infinitesimally small a part that his interests could easily be sacrificed at the altar of the public good, at the altar of society itself, because nothing was more dangerous to society than the corrosion and undermining of the very element

which held it together, that is, the faith.[75] Publicly to hold
opinions which ran counter to or attacked the faith determined and fixed by law was heresy, and the real reason
for making heresy a crime was—as Gratian's *Decretum* had
explained it[76]—that the heretic showed intellectual arrogance
by preferring his own opinions to those who were specially
qualified to pronounce upon matters of faith.[77] Consequently,
heresy was high treason, committed against the divine
majesty, committed through aberration from the faith as laid
down by the papacy.[78] Behind this thesis stood the reflection that not only had the individual no right to express
himself on matters of faith but also that faith itself was an
issue of profound public concern, for if the faith as the bond
of society were allowed to be corroded, the foundations
of society would break down and society itself would collapse.
The severe punishment meted out to heretics proved that
the principle of public utility was carried to its logical conclusion; and the confiscation of the property of the culprit
and of his descendants, even if as yet unborn, as well as the
inability to occupy public or ecclesiastical offices, is further
testimony to the fact that the individual had to suppress his
views on matters which might well have vitally affected him,

[75] From the medieval point of view this suppression of the individual's
opinion was not by any means seen as a violation of his rights or of his
dignity as a Christian, because a Christian attacking established faith
forfeited his dignity and could be considered "a bad man." Killing this
individual did not violate his dignity, just as killing an animal did not
affect anyone's dignity; see for further details my Introducton to Henry
Charles Lea, *A History of the Inquisition of the Middle Ages* (London,
1963).

[76] Gratian, xxiv. 3. 30. Hence, it was also declared that deviation from
faith was an implicit attack on Christ as "the stable and perpetual foundation" of society; see Innocent IV *Quia tunc* (in *Bullarium Romanum* iii.
584). After all, Christ was corporeally present in the pope; see Walter
Ullmann, *The Growth of Papal Government in the Middle Ages*, (2d ed.;
London, 1962), p. 444, n. 1. See further text.

[77] Aberration from faith as laid down by authority was in itself a rebellion against the legitimately constituted superior.

[78] For some details see Walter Ullmann, in *Etudes d'histoire du droit
canonique dédiées à Gabriel Le Bras* (Paris, 1965), I, 729ff.

38   *The Individual and Society*

because the good of society demanded this. Nevertheless, in stating these matters, no moral evaluation is intended; above all, it would be quite anachronistic to assess these and other similar measures by the yardstick of our modern, somewhat refined and sophisticated criteria.

In close proximity to this topic stood the relationship between the individual's property and the Ruler's right to dispose of it. It should be borne in mind that, within the framework of the descending theme of government, ultimately property was considered an issue of divine grace,[79] which view precluded the emergence of a thesis according to which the individual as owner had an autonomous right to his property.[80] Consequently, for sufficient reason property could be taken away by those who were qualified to pronounce upon the issue of grace.[81] Because of the theocratic function of the Ruler himself, a theory developed that he was in actual fact the owner of all the goods which his subjects possessed. This thesis was explicitly stated in the twelfth century by the civilian Martinus, who, commenting upon the Roman law, declared that its expression that "everything is understood to be in the prince's power" meant one thing: the Ruler was the full owner of all the property of his subjects; accordingly, he could dispose of it as he saw fit.[82] He had true *dominium*—property unrestricted and unhampered by any authority or law—precisely because he was the vicegerent of God on earth.[83]

[79] See Ullmann, *Principles of Government*, p. 76, and *History of Political Thought*, p. 113.
[80] See also Augustine as reported in Gratian, viii. 1.
[81] For this see the pronouncement by Gregory VII *Reg.* vii. 14a, ed. E. Caspar (repr. Berlin, 1960), p. 487.
[82] See the report of the *glossa ordinaria* on *Codex* vii. 37. 3 (Bene a Zenone), where the imperial law used this terminology: "cum omnia principis esse intelligantur." Other eminent jurists following this line of thought were, for instance, Ricardus Malumbra and Jacobus de Ravanis.
[83] See, for example, Albericus de Rosciate *Ia Const. Dig.* (ed. Lugduni, 1545) fol. 4vb. no. 9: "Deus est dominus omnium, ut in psalmo, 'Domini est terra et plenitudo eius', et imperator est in terris loco Dei quoad temporalia, et papa quoad spiritualia."

This logically unimpeachable thesis could be somewhat modified, however, as indicated by the interpretation of another civilian, Bulgarus, who advanced the theory that the Ruler did not own the individual's property, but was its protector. It is not difficult to see here the re-emergence of the old view of the *Munt* in the guise of the Roman legal concept of supreme protection and jurisdiction. The crucial point here is that the basis of the Ruler's right to dispose of an individual's property rested not upon his ownership, but rather upon his function as a governor or *gubernator,* who, because he was the sole judge of what furthered the public weal, the *utilitas publica,* could legally dispose of property if the public interest warranted it.[84] The general provision which covered the right of expropriation was that the Ruler have a *justa causa,* and a pre-eminently just cause evidently was the protection of the public interest,[85] which bore no relationship to the interests of the individual, who, it must be remembered, had no means of challenging the Ruler's disposition before a court of law, because the Ruler alone was credited with the special knowledge of what was in the best interests of society.[86] No constitutional or legal machinery existed to impugn the Ruler's judgment that "a

[84] See *glossa ordinaria* ad Dig. proem., s.v. "sanctionem": "Quod hic dicit, 'Omnem totius reipublicae nostrae', id est, totius imperii, quod est suum, et res in eo contentae, ratione *jurisdictionis* vel *protectionis,* non proprietatis, secundum Bulgarum, sed secundum Martinum etiam proprietatis"; ead. ad *Codex* vii. 37. 3, s.v. "omnia principis": "His expone, quoad protectionem vel jurisdictionem." See also ead. ad Dig. 1. 8. 2, s.v. "litora."

[85] See Ullmann, *Idea of Law,* pp. 185f., at n. 4 ("ratione publicae utilitatis," Lucas de Penna). Hence, no compensation for confiscated property: "maxime si propter publicam utilitatem faciat (scil. princeps)," *glossa ordinaria* ad Dig. 1. 14. 3, s.v. "multo magis." Later doctrine was inclined to impose on the Ruler some duty of paying compensation; see Baldus *Ia Const. Dig.* (Venice, 1616) fol. 4va. no. 12, s.v. "omnem": "Imperator dat precium, licet modicum. . . ."

[86] According to Jacobus Butrigarius the Ruler was not "dominus rerum singularium, nisi cura et solicitudine"; cited by Albericus de Rosciate *Ia Const. Dig.* fol. 4ra. no. 9.

just cause" demanded action.[87] The *Munt* of the Ruler was the operational instrument in this scheme, which is only another way of saying that what mattered was the well-being of society. The disregard of the interests of the individual was not a disregard of his rights—which in any case he did not autonomously have within this framework—but a sign of his complete absorption in society. His situation might be compared to that of heretics in inquisitorial proceedings, in which the overriding interest was the preservation of the faith: this *favor fidei* meant the setting aside of the ordinary modes of criminal procedure against the accused.[88] Similarly, if the interests of the whole society demanded it, property could be confiscated and transferred to some other individual: it was the *favor reipublicae* which in the last resort justified this procedure.[89]

Here another observation can be made concerning the mutual relations between society and the individual. Society was pictured as a large organism in which each member had been allotted a special function which he pursued for the common good. Two characteristic facets of medieval life are intimately linked with this consideration. First, there was the stratification of medieval society into its estates. The significance of this stratification within the present context is that it was precisely the hallmark of a member of a particular estate that he could not move out of his own estate and that whatever status he enjoyed, he was rigidly con-

---

[87] This was, for instance, explicitly stated by Albericus, *ibid.*, fol. 5ra. no. 12: "Nec erit qui dijudicare possit utrum sit justa causa vel non, quia ipse [scil. princeps] *facta subditorum* judicat, sua judicat solus Deus."

[88] About this *favor fidei* see my Introduction to Lea, *Inquisition of the Middle Ages.*

[89] This was the argument used by Albericus de Rosciate, ad Dig. 6. 1. 15. fol. 341. no. 3. Clearly enough, this whole cluster of very important problems is in urgent need of an exhaustive examination, which should focus attention on the implications of such views as those of Baldus, who distinguished between the "jus *publicum* Caesaris et *privatarum* personarum" (*Ia Const. Dig.*): Baldus, ad *Codex* vii. 37. 3. fol. 28va. no. 2, and *Codex* vii. 37. 2. fol. 28ra. no. 1.

trolled by the norms applicable to his estate. These norms concerned his very standing within society, concerned any privileges he might have had, including the right of inheritance, of marriage; in short, the norms of a particular estate contributed to the petrification of society and the ossification of the individual's status within it.[90] That the freemen and the unfree were treated fundamentally differently, especially in regard to the *Wergeld,* and that there were basic procedural differences between them need only be mentioned for one to realize how closely linked the individual was with his estate. In cases in which *Wergeld* was paid, it was neither paid nor received by the individual, but by his kindred, by his *Sippe.* Moreover, even the value of an oath depended upon the estate to which the individual taking the oath belonged.[91] "Queer arithmetical rules will teach how the oath of one thegn is as weighty as the oath of six ceorls, and the like" (Maitland). One has, furthermore, but to think of the medieval serfs such as the ploughman, the cotter, and their offsprings, et cetera, all of whom were praedial and were sold with the ground itself, if one wishes to visualize the sharp legal cleavage that existed within medieval society—a cleavage based entirely on custom and tradition, not on rational considerations. That any change in the structure of society was resisted by the "beati possidentes" is not difficult to understand.[92]

In close proximity to this feature of medieval life stood

[90] For the static complexion of medieval society resulting from the division into estates, see also Karl Bosl, "Potens und Pauper," *Alteuropa und die moderne Gesellschaft: Festschrift für Otto Brunner* (Göttingen, 1964), pp. 60ff., esp. 81ff., now also in Karl Bosl, *Frühformen der Gesellschaft im mittelalterlichen Europa* (Munich-Vienna, 1964), pp. 106ff. That even within the nobility there was, in some regions and countries, little equality of its members has been shown by Marc Bloch, *Feudal Society,* trans. L. A. Manyon (London, 1961), pp. 332ff.

[91] See Heinrich Brunner, *Deutsche Rechtsgeschichte* (Leipzig, 1906–28), I, 346; II, 528ff.

[92] See Rudolf Buchner in Fritz Kern, *Gottesgnadentum und Widerstandsrecht* (2d ed.; Darmstadt, 1954), p. 276, n. 282.

another, and it was that each member of society should fulfill the functions which were allotted to him, because this was held to have been the effluence of the divine ordering of things. It was the principle of vocation—in the last resort traceable to Christian cosmology—according to which every individual had been called (*vocatus*) to fulfill specific tasks. *Unusquisque maneat in ea vocatione in qua dignoscitur vocatus* (Everybody should abide in that calling to which he is known to have been called) was often said in adapting the Pauline exhortation[93] to the medieval structure of society. This view expressed the functional ordering within society as well as the vocational stratification of society and became a virtually insuperable stumbling block to the release of the individual's own faculties.

Secondly, the medieval viewpoint that each individual had a specific function which he pursued for the common good had a rather distinguished pedigree. It was Paul who used the human body as a model in order to demonstrate the various functions within the *unum corpus christi*.[94] This organological or anthropomorphic thesis meant that each part of the human body functioned for the sake of the whole, not for its own sake. If we translate this into terms of the corporate public body, we are here presented with the theory that the individual did not exist for his own sake, but for the sake of the whole society. This organological thesis was to lead in time to the full-fledged integration theory of the corporate body politic, in which the individual is wholly submerged in society for the sake of the well-being of society itself.[95] This thesis also led without undue effort to the allegory of the head's directing the other parts of the human body, thus metaphorically expressing the superior function

[93] I Cor. 7:20, where the term *vocatio* seems to have been used for the first time.

[94] See I Cor. 12:4ff.; Eph. 1:23; Rom. 12:5.

[95] For the application of the Pauline organological thesis by John of Salisbury, see Ullmann, *History of Political Thought*, p. 124.

of the *caput*—be this king or pope—and the inferior position of the subject individual. The essential point of this organological thesis is that although the body public was one and indivisible, in which all its members had to play their role, it nevertheless needed authoritative guidance by the head and, thus, the law "given from above." The closely integrated structure of society called forth the monarchic principle, the underlying idea being that the members of society were not fit enough to guide society, which was entrusted to the Ruler's government. The primary concern was the good of society, of the whole body of subjects, and not of the individuals. In a roundabout way we return to the *utilitas publica,* which is to be preferred to the *utilitas privata.*

An adequate assessment of the medieval point of view must stress a feature which runs right through governmental actions, writings, speeches, sermons, tracts, pictorial representations, in fact any product of the creative mind. This is a feature which is perhaps difficult for us to grasp today, but which seems to me essential if one wishes to penetrate the medieval texture. We are today so easily inclined to put the individual in the forefront and, in assessing him, to proceed by largely subjective criteria. This is especially marked in historical writings about the more recent period. That such a *modus procedendi* harbors all the dangers of a moral evaluation and purely subjective assessment sometimes degenerating into national if not nationalistic appraisal is in no need of emphasis.

Precisely because the individual in the Middle Ages was submerged in society, there is very little danger of these personal, subjective methods of assessment asserting themselves. It is assuredly not without coincidence that we know so very little of the personal traits of most of the men who directed the path of medieval society. Hardly any personal correspondence has survived; no personal anecdotes are there; none of the stories which grow round great men exists; there are few biographical data; above all, there is hardly any worthwhile contemporary biography or pictorial representation of the great kings, popes, or emperors. Is it not rather symptomatic that we have no pictures which indicate how Nicholas I or Gregory VII or Louis I or Henry II looked? I think it is the lack of knowing the individuality of medieval personalities which explains, to a certain extent at least, why historical writings concerned with the Middle Ages are sometimes quite radically different from historical writings concerned with the more recent periods.

What mattered was not the individual, was not the man, but, as I have already implied, the office which that individual occupied. The office itself is capable of precise measurement, capable of a purely objective assessment: it can be measured by its own contents. It was the office which absorbed the individual, but the office and the power it contained were not of human origin or making, but of allegedly divine provenance. Once again, we move within a-human, non-individualistic precincts. Sculpture and portraiture in the high Middle Ages reveal the same features. However finely executed are the illuminations in medieval manuscripts of the Reichenau or Canterbury schools, for example, the men depicted there are not real men at all, but merely types. All individuality is absent. The explanation seems clear enough: the individual personality was not yet seen in its multifarious, infinitely subtle variations. The artist did not lack ability, assuredly not, but what he lacked was the perception of the distinguishing features of the individual he portrayed. On the other hand, however, these same illuminations show that the artist took infinite pains to depict the garments and paraphernalia of the office which his subject occupied. He also devoted great attention to any symbolic gestures or symbolic elements or ritual features which, once again, spoke a purely objective language, a language which was unambiguous and easily comprehensible.

This objective point of view can also be witnessed with unmistakable clarity in the historiography of the Middle Ages. Why is it, one is, I think, entitled to ask, that medieval historiography is so impersonal? Why is it that we can deduce so little from the purely annalistic accounts, from the *Gesta,* the *Annales,* the *Chronica,* and so forth? All of these seem to me largely variations of one and the same theme. I think it is not always appreciated that so many chronicles start with the creation of the world, that is, the book of Genesis. This fact seems to me a rather clear pointer to the nature of medieval historiography, for the annalist or chronicler did not see in the succession of events the play of human volitions and aims, but the manifestations of God's will. The individual was only involved in the historical process so far as he was conceived as an instrument, as a vehicle through which God acted. In other words, history seen through the eyes of the medieval annalist was believed to have revealed the divine plan, was a process removed from the individual's capacity, and the real task of the annalist or chronicler was to uncover the objective divine plan. At most the individual could only further the divine plan or perhaps impede it, but he never made the plan himself.[96] That, I think, explains why we find in medieval historiography so little account taken of the actual human, individual features and motives. Everything moved, so to speak, on the objective level of a

---

[96] Comparing Gregory of Tours and his Roman models, Karl Langosch, *Profile des lateinischen Mittelalters* (Darmstadt, 1965), p. 36, pertinently remarks that the Romans "zeigen nur ein sachliches Interesse an Politik und Kriegsführung, leiten das Geschehen nur aus *menschlichen* Kräften und Trieben her und sind von einer ganz *diesseitigen* Weltanschauung erfüllt. Bei Gregor dagegen dominiert von der ersten bis zur letzten Zeile ein völlig christliches Denken. Gott und die Heiligen lenken die Geschichte, dass sich die christlichen Gebote schon auf Erden durchsetzen." (Italics mine.) See also pp. 30, 43, 123ff. (Paulus Diaconus).

divine plan, on a level which purposely disregarded the
importance of the individual's own contributions, if not his
own initiative. The individual could be compared to a chess-
man which was moved by divinity across the chess board
of historical events. Moreover, there was little separation
between the miraculous and the historical. Miracles and
legends took the place of rational explanation by means of
cause and effect. Being embedded in the divine plan, history
was its manifestation in the period between the creation and
the day of judgment. That so much of medieval historiography was teleologically conceived and that one can very
well speak of a teleology of history itself would seem to be
evident.[97]

Basically, the medieval viewpoint concerning the standing
of the individual in society was the result of the combination
of two fundamental themes, to both of which I have tried to
give due emphasis: the overriding importance of law in the
Middle Ages and the organological conception of society,
which latter was nothing less than the Pauline clothing for
the Roman corporation thesis. Although the properly medieval doctrine did not and could not give us a thesis of the
autonomous standing of the individual in society, it nonetheless bequeathed to the modern world a principle which is not,
even today, fully implemented in a number of societies,
specifically, the rule of law. Every medievalist is familiar
with the allegory of soul and body, with the *anima* which
ruled the *corpus*.[98] This is usually taken to mean the higher
value of the soul and the lower value of the body; sometimes

---

[97] About this topic see also *Geschichtsdenken und Geschichtsbild im
Mittelalter*, ed. W. Lammers (Darmstadt, 1965), especially the contributions by Johannes Spörl, pp. 1ff., and Herbert Grundmann, pp. 418ff.

[98] It is interesting that Augustine operated with the antithesis of mind
and flesh when he expressed a similar point of view. To the question of
what order consisted of, he replied: "God commands the mind (soul), the
mind commands the flesh (body), and there cannot be anything more
orderly than this arrangement," *Miscellanea Agostiniana*, Vol. I. *Sermones
post Maurinos reperti* (Rome, 1930), p. 633, ll. 17–19. For another
statement of his to the same effect, see *ibid.*, n. 18.

the soul was equated with the mind, and the body with matter. This is not incorrect, nor is it incorrect to explain the metaphor by saying that the soul was the symbol of priesthood and the body the symbol of kingship. In a syllogistic way it was frequently asserted that just as the soul ruled the body, in the same way the priesthood ruled the laity and kings.

I think, however, that this allegory has considerably more ideological significance than is usually given it.[99] Transposed to a more general level, the point of substance in the allegory of soul and body—which indeed is pre-Christian and originated in Hellenistic thought[100]—is that the law was the soul, because it was the *norma recte vivendi,* because it was the norm of the right order of living. The law, as the soul, ruled the corporate entity, ruled the body, be it the Church or a kingdom or an empire. When we read in the Visigothic Laws of the seventh century that

Lex est *anima* totius *corporis* popularis,[101]

we have pretty clear proof of how strongly entrenched was the idea of law as the regulating and animating force of society, even at that early time. It was an idea that in varying keys was repeated over and over throughout the Middle Ages, down to the seventeenth century, when Spinoza declared that

Anima enim *imperii jura* sunt: his igitur servatis servatur necessario imperium.[102]

---

[99] I have made some preliminary observations on this topic in my *Principles of Government,* pp. 92f.; *History of Political Thought,* p. 101; and in the *Atti Primo Congresso Internazionale di Storia del Diritto,* I (1965), but I think I can now go a little further.

[100] See, for instance, Isocrates *Areopagitikos* 7. 14 (ed. Loeb Classical Library, 1929, p. 112); Demosthenes *Against Timocrates* 210 (ed. *ibid.,* 1936, p. 508); Sextus Empiricus *Against the Professors* ii. 31 (ed. *ibid.,* 1949, p. 205).

[101] M.G.H., *Leges Visigothorum* i. 2. 2.

[102] Benedict de Spinoza *Tractatus Politicus* x. 9, ed. A. G. Wernham (Oxford, 1958), p. 436.

Indeed, this medieval standpoint would demonstrate that the soul (in this allegory) was the medieval precursor of the idea of the *Rechtsstaat*, of the supremacy of law, of the rule of law. The prevalent legalism of the Middle Ages which took so little account of the individual seems to me incontrovertible proof of the thesis that only through the instrumentality of the law could a public body live, develop, and reach its end. The soul was considered the vivifying organ of the individual; in the same way the soul, conceived as the law, breathed life into, or *animated*, the public body.

Because the individual played an insignificant role within the descending theme of government and law, the medieval apotheosis of the law becomes easily accessible to understanding. What mattered was, as I have been at pains to show, not the individual, but society, the corpus of all individuals. In the high Middle Ages, thinking in the public field concerned itself with the whole, with society. But law at all times and in all societies addresses itself to the generality, to the multitude and, by definition, sets aside the individual.[103] One might be inclined to say that the medieval emphasis on the collectivist phenomenon of the law successfully prevented the emergence of a thesis concerning such rights which the individual had had apart from the law and before the law was given. The theme of the law as the soul of the body (public and politic) was, in other words, explicable by the overriding importance attached to society and by the negligible role which the individual played in it. Differently expressed, the collectivist trend of thought gave rise, at least embryonically, to the incipient thesis of the idea of the rule of law, a standpoint upon which all shades of opinion in the Middle Ages were agreed. The law was the invisible Ruler of society, made concrete by the visible

[103] This also emerged with unmistakable clarity in the Visigothic Laws of the seventh century, when they declared that the legislator issued law "nullo privatim commodo, sed *omnium civium utilitati communi,*" ibid., i. 1. 3.

Ruler,[104] who disposed of both *scientia* and *potestas*, who, in a word, knew what justice and the interests of the society in his charge demanded. One might well be tempted to speak of a nomocratic conception which impressed itself upon the Middle Ages, an amalgam of Hellenistic, Roman, and Christian elements.[105] It is, I think, only from this standpoint that one can understand the often repeated declaration (hardly heeded by modern medievalists) that the Ruler himself was the embodied idea of law, was the *nomos empsychos,* the *lex animata.*

The recognition which we now have also makes understandable the theme of immortality or sempiternity of public bodies, precisely because the law was their soul. Because the soul was said to be immortal, public bodies, which were what they were through the law, could also not die and were credited, therefore, with sempiternity. In a roundabout way we return to the collectivist standpoint—all the individual bodies may and will die, but what cannot die is the idea of law, the idea of right order, which holds the public and corporate body together and which, therefore, possessed sempiternity. I believe it was Alexis de Tocqueville who, in reference to the law, once said that "governments may perish, but society cannot die." By virtue of seeing in the concept of the soul the purest idea of law and right, medieval doctrine took a very great step forward. Although the modern concept of the individual endowed with full, autonomous, independent, and indigenous rights in society was the result of a development which challenged the properly medieval doctrine, this doctrine, by virtue of its collectivist, nomo-

---

[104] According to the same Visigothic laws, the law obtains force ("valorem obtineat") "in *cunctis personis* ac *gentibus* nostrae amplitudinis imperio subjugatis innexum sibi a nostra gloria . . ." *ibid.,* ii. 1. 1.

[105] See also above, n. 12. For the role of the *nomos* in Hellenistic political philosophy, see Victor Ehrenberg, *Der Staat der Griechen* (Stuttgart, 1965), p. 215: "Aus dem unpersönlichen König Nomos, der die Polis als Rechtsstaat regierte, war der in der Person des Königs verkörperte Nomos geworden."

cratic character, nevertheless firmly implanted the idea of the supremacy of the law in the Western mind, not in spite of, but—the paradox is merely apparent—because of the absence of any thesis of autonomous rights on the part of the individual. We shall see, I hope, how important this bequest of the Middle Ages was for the development of the modern *Rechtsstaat;* the descending theme of government and law, with its concomitant lack of the individual's standing in society, was only one phase, but a very important one, in the weary history of the relations between man and society.

II

THE PRACTICAL THESIS

The Constitutional Significance of the
Feudal Relationship and Its Bearing on
the Individual in Society

1

There is some justification, I think, for saying that the followers of medieval doctrine—the basic elements of which I tried to present in my first lecture—were confined, to a very large extent, to what might be called the upper strata of society. The descending theme of government and law found its most notable manifestation in official expressions of governments and in the works of littérateurs, the latter especially in the writings of the Masters at the universities. It was only a rather thin upper crust of society in which the purely abstract doctrine had gained a firm foothold.

Looking somewhat lower down the social scale and trying to put our ears, so to speak, to the ground, we may detect some features which would show how little in actual fact the broad masses of medieval society were affected by the somewhat rarefied speculative doctrines. The fact remains, however, that although one might well be tempted to doubt not only the correctness but also the actual social relevance of that pure doctrine which saw the individual merely as a recipient of favors and which gave him no constitutional standing or autonomous function within society itself, it is, I think, rather necessary to recognize the gulf separating government and governed, a gulf easily recognizable precisely because the individual had not been accorded the status of a citizen. There was not merely a social stratification virtually amounting to an isolation between the two estates on the one hand and the rest of mankind on the other hand; there was also a quite noticeable distinction concerning the conduct of affairs in the socially privileged ranks of society and in the lower regions.

If one wishes to understand why and how it came about that from the late thirteenth century the individual gradually emerged as a full-fledged citizen, it would seem profitable to look at two rather practical facets of medieval society: on the one hand, the manner in which those far away from the gaze of official governments conducted their own affairs and, on the other hand, the feudal form of government which was practiced all over Europe. Neither of these two was founded upon any clear-cut, neat, and tidy theory such as described in the first lecture. What we are presented with is practice without high-flown theory, doing without much intellectual reflexion, activity without speculation and without the always somehow embarrassing question as to whether or not facts could be squared with theorems and ideas. Similarly, we cannot expect learned treatises, tracts, and books, because to a large extent those who conducted their affairs "down below"—if I may use such metaphorical language—were hardly fit and educated enough to put their thoughts and ideas into scholarly writings. From a wider historical viewpoint, however, it seems to me that those practical aspects deserve considerably more emphasis than medieval scholarship has so far accorded to them. Without them it would seem to me well-nigh impossible to explain why there was the somewhat radical change toward the end of the thirteenth century, a change that in more than one respect ushered in the period which we like to call modern.

Despite the insistent and repeated proclamation of the descending theme of government and law, with its corollary of the individual as a mere subject, and despite the equally insistently repeated assertion that this was the only way in which the individual fitted into the christocentric system of government, the hierarchically lower placed sections of the populace acted in a manner which to all intents and purposes was far from implementing those speculative theses. Precisely because there was a gulf between the "higher and lower regions," it would appear not only that the somewhat rarefied doctrines propounded within the former failed to reach the latter, but also that extremely little effort was in fact made to extend theory and speculation to the illiterate and uneducated sections. Further, because the villein, the cotter, the crofter, the plowman, the bailiff, the miller, and so on, were so far below the vision of the "learned" circles and the attention of governments, they were able to conduct their business with little intervention by those set above them. Parenthetically, the question is at least justified: How much of an impact did the allegedly biblically based and theoretically conceived speculations, the medieval Christian governmental doctrine, make upon the "less privileged," upon the broad masses of the populace? It is always dangerous to conclude that what an official decree or law or writing contained corresponded to the accepted assumptions of all the sections of society itself. It appears, in fact, that the "lower" section—in reality a *quantité negligeable* from the governmental point of view—seemed in a most unsophisticated manner to take for granted that the individual had precisely those rights which the abstract descending thesis of government had denied him. It may not be too great a risk to express the opinion that what was done by the unsophisticated, predominantly agricultural section of the populace was far more germane, more natural to the ordinary men and women, than the implementation of highly esoteric doctrine by governments and the propounding of it by writers. I have no hesitation in saying that it was the reality of transacting public business—if I may use so great a name for quite primitive activities—by the lower reaches of the community which, in conjunction with the feudal form of government, was to provide some secure foundation for the later emergence of the doctrine of the individual as a full-grown citizen.

One or two examples should make clear this contention. To begin with, there were throughout the Middle Ages numerous associations, unions, fraternities, guilds, and communities which in one way or another considered the individual a full member.[1] What these truly numberless associations exhibit is the urge of individuals to combine into larger groups: partly for reasons of self-protection, partly for reasons of mutual insurance, partly for reasons of pursuing sectional interests, these unions were to all intents and purposes communities which provided for the individual the security which he otherwise would have lacked. What is immediately important, however, is that the members themselves elected their own officers and, above all, made their own regulations, managed their own affairs. The villages in particular furnish good illustrations, for they arranged the times of plowing, tilling, and cultivating the soil, the time of harvesting, and the manner of policing the fields. The use of rivers, wells, brooks, waterways, and, in general, the utilization of pastoral land, compensation for damage to crops by fire or straying cattle, and so forth, were determined by the villagers themselves. In the village potteries, smithies, tileries, quarries, et cetera, working conditions were laid down by the village community itself. In other words, we have here a "system" at work which shows all the characteristic features of the ascending theme of government and law, according to which original power resided in the members of the community, in the individuals themselves.

What needs emphasis in this context is that the villagers themselves were held to be, and constituted themselves as, full members of the village community, a viewpoint which

---

[1] For some tentative observations in this respect see Ullmann, *Principles of Government*, pp. 215ff., and *History of Political Thought*, pp. 160f.

had at least two important consequences: first, the idea of equality, the idea that they as members of the community were equals, found some practical application[2] entailing also economic consequences; secondly, village self-government became a practical measure not suggested by any theory, not initiated "from above," not legislated by a "superior," but practiced as a "natural" way of conducting the business of the village.[3] It is not surprising, therefore, that the husbandry of the village was regulated by the village community itself, "by a set of rules binding upon all the villagers,"[4] because every villager had a means to express his views on matters which concerned him and in which he had a legitimate interest. One might go as far as to say that the Roman law dictum "what touches all must be approved by all" was evolved and applied within the village community, although the assumption may fairly be made that the villagers had heard neither of Roman law nor of this principle. In other words, the idea of consent was very much in the forefront— in somewhat stark contrast to its absence in "great matters of State." The villagers were, so to speak, acting as full citizens—if one may employ this highly polished concept— precisely because they themselves took an active part in the "commonwealth" of the village government. That they elected their "officers" is not, therefore, difficult to understand;[5] that, moreover, the "office" to which the reeve, the blacksmith, the hayward, and the other functionaries were elected was delineated and circumscribed by the electors fits perfectly into the mental framework within which the

[2] See George C. Homans, *English Villagers of the Thirteenth Century* (Cambridge, Mass., 1942), p. 337; further, John P. Dawson, *A History of Lay Judges* (Cambridge, Mass., 1960), p. 281; see now also especially Karl S. Bader, *Dorfgemeinschaft und Dorfgemeinde im Mittelalter* (Cologne and Graz, 1962), II, 270f.

[3] Homans, *English Villagers*, p. 331.

[4] *Ibid.*, p. 290.

[5] See especially Bader, *Dorfgemeinschaft und Dorfgemeinde*, pp. 364–66.

villagers acted.[6] (Once again we notice the contrast to the "high offices of State," which were, so to speak, laid up in heaven.) Consequently, the idea of representation, which, within the descending theme of government, could never make its appearance, was acted upon and observed as a matter of self-evident course. True enough, there were, within the village community, three "social classes" discernible—the franklins, the husbonds, the cotters[7]—and although they might conceivably approximate the three estates,[8] they never manifested the harsh and sharp cleavages of the latter. There was, to be sure, social distinction, but no legally or constitutionally enforceable separation. To all practical intents and purposes the villager counted as an individual and, in the "public" sphere, as a citizen.

It was this separation with its firmly established barriers which made it so excruciatingly difficult to cross from one estate into another, a difficulty which hardly existed within the village and which, moreover, could be eliminated by the ease with which the villager could change his personal status when he migrated into a town. *Stadtluft macht frei* was an acknowledgment of the emancipation of the villager from his village community, but it was also more: the migration into a town enabled him to change his social status and, thereby, to rise also in his "political" status, as a merchant might "graduate" into an economically as well as politically different estate altogether. The towns themselves exhibited features which were in many respects not dissimilar to the villages, namely self-government and autonomy of their own legislation.

The town council itself pointed toward the full weight

---

[6] *Ibid.*, p. 366, especially in connection with supervision of water supply (important for firefighting services); police duties; supervision of weights and measures; trade, particularly baking, milling, brick making, and so on.

[7] Homans, *English Villagers*, p. 242.

[8] See *ibid.*, p. 245.

which the individual members had in regard to the government of the town and the management of civic affairs. In a quite different context Stubbs many years ago drew attention to the self-government of the towns which elected their own provost or gerefa and bydel (bedel) and bailiffs and had their own courts. It was also in the towns that the guilds and fraternities and sodalities proliferated—once again, an unmistakable sign that the merchants and journeymen and artisans were quite untouched by the sophisticated thesis of the individual as a mere recipient of the law. Both the town and the guilds made their own regulations, and one need not be too cautious in seeing these regulations as the law proper, at least as far as they themselves were concerned. In other words, the law was not given to them, but made by them, and from a jurisprudential point of view it is a matter of some concern to discern here the vital element —so conspicuously absent within the theocratic thesis—the element of consent.

Here is, I think, the point at which some passing reference to the all-pervading customary law in the Middle Ages is called for. Customary law was not the outcome of a deliberate enactment by a superior law-giver, but was the result of usages and practices which by common consent were based on tacit agreement—it was a law which manifested a common interest of those who in the first instance gave birth to the usages and practices observed among them. As a matter of fact, it would seem that customary law had far greater importance for the ordinary men and women than the still somewhat isolated legislative enactments by popes, kings, and emperors. The matters concerning ordinary, daily life were ruled by custom, a circumstance observable still in modern times, for anyone today only slightly familiar with the way in which the peasants in different Alpine districts live and regulate their lives will confirm the variety and resilience of their customs. Virtually every department of medieval social life was subjected to the customary usages, which, because they were old and of unknown origin, were not only held to be good, but also—and above all—binding upon all members of a community. From the jurisprudential angle the essential points are that customary law was a law that was based upon the consent of the individuals themselves—at least by way of construction—and that this law had nothing to do with the law given by superior authority.

It is, therefore, not difficult to understand that conceptually the all-pervasive customary law constituted a danger to the efficacy of the descending theme of government. The gulf to which I have referred could also be seen, most drastically, in the two systems of law, the unwritten, customary law, and the written, enacted law given by the superior. As long as customary law moved, so to speak, within the precincts of the written law and merely amplified it, no serious problem could and did arise. It was altogether different, however, if customary law opposed written law. It was in this context that scholars and writers and governments were bound to take notice of customary law. It is not without interest that the Code of Justinian contained a law issued by Constantine the Great according to which customary law could not display such validity as to abrogate any imperial, that is, enacted law.[9] The problem, consequently, was: How could the prevalent and practiced customary law conceptually be fitted into the equally prevalent theoretical system of the descending theme of government? It stands to reason that customary law could not be abolished or eliminated or even reduced in its efficacy, and yet it was, to put it no lower, a thorn in the flesh of any descending kind of government.

The construction chosen was a fiction and, therefore, satisfied the theoreticians no less than the governments. The Ruler, it was maintained, by virtue of his legislative omnipotence, could have opposed customary law, but by not

[9] *Cod. Just.* viii. 52. 2.

opposing it, he gave at least tacit approval to it. In this way he could be said to have confirmed the validity and efficacy of customary law.[10] No small amount of assistance was provided by the statement in Roman law—also adopted by canon law—that the prince has all the laws in his breast. It was a thesis which, applied to the problem of how to fit customary law into the framework of the descending theme of government, saved the Ruler's face as well as customary law. It was a thesis which soothed troubled juristic consciences, yet did not upset the traditional efficacy of customary law, a law, I must repeat, which for practical purposes was far more important than the law given by a superior, and a law which, closely scrutinized, exposed the purely theoretical character of the descending theme of government and law. But medieval theoreticians were never at a loss to find a way out of an impasse.

What, above all, makes customary law so important in my context is that it was a law which resulted overwhelmingly from the activities of lay individuals, for in the lower strata of medieval society it was the lay people who figured prominently. Their degree of importance was dependent, in part, on their educational attainments, which differed widely in various regions in Western Europe; and the educational standards of individuals must, as I mentioned in my first lecture, be properly assessed in precisely the matters which are here of concern. In twelfth-century Italy, for example, the layman had a considerable educational advantage over

---

[10] See, e.g., the *glossa ordinaria* on *ibid.*: customary law was valid, because "princeps patitur ex certa scientia" and "quia princeps scire *fingitur* et sic consentire." The same *glossa ordinaria* speaks here also of the "patientia principis permittentis." See, furthermore, the gloss of Irnerius, printed in Friedrich K. Savigny, *Geschichte des römischen Rechts im Mittelalter* (Heidelberg, 1852), IV, 458f. Others, such as Lucas de Penna, went even further and declared that toleration of customary law by the prince was insufficient and that it had to be introduced with the knowledge and approval of the prince; see the passage cited in Ullmann, *Idea of Law*, p. 64.

the layman in, say, the Low Countries or in Saxony. It is not really surprising that the communal movement, with its marked participation of the lay individuals in public affairs, manifested itself so strongly in Northern Italy long before there was a similar movement north of the Alps, which indeed never reached Italian dimensions and significance.

Far be it from me to suggest that these and similar expressions of the communal will would show that lower social strata harbored anything even faintly approaching the thesis of the individual's full rights in the public field, but what I would maintain is that they provided, so to speak, a subterranean, invisible platform which was to prove of not inconsiderable assistance in the process of emancipating the individual, a mere subject, from the restricted role into which doctrine had cast him. The paradoxical situation emerged that the customary practices and usages in the lower strata assumed great historic significance, although the layman, precisely because he was a layman, was held by doctrine to be incapable of taking part in government and in the making of the law, the reason being that he lacked the appropriate knowledge, that he did not possess *scientia*. It was this lack, we may recall, which was said to make him unsuitable, unqualified for the role of a member participating in government. In other words, one of the important bridges between the abstract medieval thesis and the subsequent humanistic thesis was the practical deployment of the individual's capabilities mainly in the lower regions of society, capabilities of the very individual whom current doctrine had dubbed an *idiota*,[11] whose lack of knowledge rendered him unsuitable and unqualified to partake in public government.

[11] This terminology goes back to the second century; see George H. Williams in *The Layman in Christian History*, ed. Stephen Charles Neill and Hans-Ruedi Weber (London, 1963), p. 41.

2

Let me now turn to my second and main topic, the feudal theme, feudal practice, and feudal law. Although feudalism, as far as its origins can be discerned in the misty past, was the result of social, agricultural, and, above all, military circumstances, and although it would have seemed too sterile to become the carrier, if not the begetter, of some of the most influential views relating to the individual himself, the fact remains that once the feudal arrangement had lost its original military trappings, it became a perfectly workable, viable, and practical system of government in which the individual was accorded some considerable standing. It was a standing which the individual had by virtue of the operations of the institution itself, by virtue of the mechanics inherent in the feudal idea and its practical application. It is not really difficult to understand why feudal practice was destined to become one of the most fruitful social and political arrangements which Western man—perhaps in a fit of absence of mind—had created, for what characterized the system was a strong bond between the feudal lord and feudal vassal, a bond that was first forged by military and social necessity and later solemnized by the oath of fealty, a bond that became so strong, resilient, and enduring, so flexible and adjustable, precisely because it was a personal as well as legal relationship. There were rights and duties on both sides: the lord had rights and duties against the vassal, and the vassal had rights and duties against the lord. It is essential to bear in mind this quite simple legal relationship involving the two individuals, for the contractual nature of feudalism became in course of time the very substratum from which some highly pregnant themes grew. Feudalism operated by forging first strong individual ties which in themselves created, in course of time, equally strong social bonds. At all times an intimate relationship between the two individuals was predominant.

The very fact that there was a contract between the two individuals, a legal bond with mutual rights and duties, meant in the first place that within the feudal precincts there was some kind of equilibrium between lord and vassal, conditioned as this was by the reciprocity of obligations. It seems to me essential to keep the reciprocal nature of the obligations in the forefront of our considerations: the feudal contract between lord and vassal produced mutual, not one-sided, obligations. Perhaps you recall that in my first lecture I referred to the absence of any right of resistance within the descending theme of government—an absence wholly understandable on its own premises. Here within the feudal sphere, however, there was a perfectly legal means of resist-ing a feudal lord who had become a tyrant: feudal practice itself, without any sophisticated theories or doctrines, had devised its own means, that of *diffidatio,* the repudiation of the feudal contract by the vassal if the lord did not fulfill his duties and went beyond the contractual bonds. By the same token a vassal, not being a subject, could not commit the crime of high treason against his lord, an offence which only a subject was capable of perpetrating.[12]

The *diffidatio* is a feature which, by virtue of the contrac-tual element, I am inclined to think, had suggested itself as the natural remedy against breach of contract, because the very essence of a contract is that both parties abide by its stipulations. Furthermore, because loyalty was one of the elements of the contract, disloyalty on one part was sufficient

[12] See, for instance, *Tractatus Universi Iuris* (Venice, 1617) xi–1. 108: "Qui a jurisdictione imperii exempti sunt, in ea conditione non sunt, ut laedere majestatem eius possint, etiamsi imperii vasalli sint. Nam vasallus non subditus est, etiamsi domino rebellis esse possit, tamen si subditus non sit, crimen laesae majestatis committere non potest." See also *ibid.,* 48v: "Feudum non dat imperium domino feudi in feudatarium; concessio feudi enim est quidam contractus, in quo aliquis obligatur, non autem imperium concedit."

reason for canceling the contract. The very idea of *diffidatio* contains as an integral element the concept of *fides*, for *diffidatio* is nothing less nor more than the withdrawal of loyalty from the lord by the vassal.[13] This loyalty was not institutionalized, but was intensely personal: it was the bond which kept lord and vassal together and had reference exclusively to the lord as an individual person. In contrast to the descending theme of government, one is here presented with a definite individual-personal relationship, that kind of relationship which, by virtue of the institutionalization of faith, could not and did not exist in the descending form of government, in which not the individual but the office constituted the essential ingredient.

It can readily be understood that the concept of loyalty or, for that matter, disloyalty is a somewhat elusive and elastic notion. For the keeping of the contract a good deal of mutual understanding and agreement—which could not be circumscribed exactly and precisely within firmly fixed and tight terms—was a necessary prerequisite. These tacit assumptions upon which the feudal arrangements and the feudal compact were based imparted to the feudal contract considerable flexibility and elasticity, and they left, of course, plenty of margin for the adjustment to newly arising contingencies and situations. One thing seems clear, and that is that the feudal arrangement, at whatever level it was practiced, of necessity presupposed the responsibility of the individual. It was not just a matter of receiving a command or a law, but it was necessary to employ one's own critical faculties. Facts, situations, circumstances, ways of means, and so forth—all had to be weighed and assessed properly if lord and vassal were to co-operate, if, in other words, the system were to work at all. Being of so individual a charac-

---

[13] See Marc Bloch, "Les formes de la rupture de l'hommage dans l'ancien droit féodal," *Revue historique de droit français et étranger,* XXXVI (1912), 141ff.; Heinrich Mitteis, *Der Staat des hohen Mittelalters* (2d ed.; Weimar, 1944), pp. 68f.; Bloch, *Feudal Society,* pp. 227ff.

ter, the actual working of the feudal compact entailed a good deal of give-and-take. It seems obvious that this arrangement considerably fostered the individual's own judgment; in fact, it presupposed and demanded it and, thereby, would appear to have become in practice one of the progenitors of the individual's own rights. In all this we shall not forget that these feudal arrangements were of native growth, were prompted by the exigencies of place and time, were, in a word, man-made. It was an intensely practical working arrangement burdened very little, if at all, by the stultifying and accumulated weight of principles, dogmas, and authority. On the contrary, feudal principles were not imposed upon society "from above," but developed gradually by slowly taking into account the actual social exigencies.[14]

All this can be demonstrated, I believe, with convincing clarity if we allow ourselves a glance at the way in which a feudally inspired government worked. One preliminary point: it has only fairly recently been recognized that, in order to understand kingship in the Middle Ages, one cannot speak of "The King" without further qualification. One must divide kingship into two parts:[15] first, there was the king by the grace of God—the theocratic king *par excellence*—who, because he alone had received the power to rule from God, stood above his subjects (symbolized by the elevated throne), who could not call him to account; secondly, next to this theocratic function every medieval king was also a feudal lord. In many vital respects this feudal function was diametrically opposed to the theocratic function; thus, every medieval king was an amphibious creature, because as a

[14] Marc Bloch, "European Feudalism," *Theories of Society,* ed. Talcot Parsons, Edward Shils *et al.* (New York, 1961), I, 385f., has very effectively drawn attention to this evolutionary feature of feudalism.

[15] For some remarks on this topic, see Walter Ullmann, "Law and the medieval Historian," *Rapports au XI Congrès International des Sciences Historiques* (Stockholm, 1960), III, 34ff., at 58ff.; *Principles of Government,* pp. 150ff.; *History of Political Thought,* pp. 145f. See also Mitteis, *Staat,* p. 491.

theocratic king his will alone counted, while as a feudal king he had entered into contractual relations of an individual nature with his tenants-in-chief and thereby had become one of them. In this feudal capacity he did not stand above the kingdom, but was a member of the feudal community itself. It was the contractual nature of the feudal compact which made the king harbor in his breast two fundamentally divergent functions. There was indeed a dichotomy within the king, a dichotomy which brooked no compromise.

Considering the centuries-long feudal practice in Western Europe and its undoubted influence, it is—and I say this with greatest diffidence and respect—a matter of some concern that medieval research has concentrated so little upon the crucially important feudal framework of society, which should be classed as a rather potent harbinger of "modern" ideas of government. Feudal law, feudal conceptions, feudal government, feudal justice—all are consigned to oblivion in dusty volumes and treated like a stepmother treats her stepchildren, yet this feudal side was of infinitely greater practical concern to contemporary society than was the abstract, conceptual point of view. What is at least as important is that the feudal mechanics had profound repercussions upon succeeding generations, which to a large extent shaped their outlook, government, and constitutional arrangements in accordance with the feudal past. We must not forget that feudal conceptions engendered their own social habits and usages; feudal justice created its own principles and, above all, was instrumental in bringing about something which might well be called feudal civilization.

Admittedly, the contrast between theory and practice is particularly marked here—the theoreticians may be likened to the well-groomed, flawlessly dressed gentlemen who frequented the drawing rooms of high-class society, while the practical men stood in the fields, had muddy boots, and showed none of the refinements of the theoreticians and could not—nor did they wish to—dazzle their contemporaries and their modern successors with the gymnastics and acrobatics of intellectual feats. What one overlooks so easily is that the bulk of medieval records comes from the theoreticians, who themselves belonged to this upper stratum of society, while the practicians left few records. That our picture of historical reality may thus be blurred seems evident. Surely it stands to reason, however, that an intensely practical form of government, such as feudalism created, struck far deeper roots than any theory, however beautifully constructed it was, could ever hope to do.

With regret, therefore, I can only state that modern research has taken so little cognizance of the historic importance of the feudal form of government. It is, nevertheless, especially gratifying on this very occasion to pay respectful tribute to one of the great medievalists of this country and an illustrious Master at this University, to the late Sidney Painter, who, with a sureness of touch and an insight which reveals the caliber of the real historian, has frequently drawn attention to the potent influence of feudal conceptions upon the making of civilized, that is, constitutional government. When Painter said that "the fundamental features of the feudal system passed into our political tradition"[16] or when he declared that "individual liberty was part of the fundamental law" which was of feudal origin, to my mind he did indeed put his finger on a basic point, namely that neither the English constitution nor the Declaration of 1776 nor the American Constitution could be understood without giving full weight to the impact which feudal conceptions, precisely because they were so intensely practical, had made upon generation after generation.

For within the feudal function of kingship, law as the vehicle of government was arrived at by counsel and consent, hence, by co-operation leading to teamwork, which was

[16] Sidney Painter, *Feudalism and Liberty* (Baltimore, 1961), p. 253.

prompted, if not necessitated, by the individual and personal relationship between the king as feudal lord and his tenants-in-chief. The essential point here is that law, as Maitland has already pointed out, was a joint effort between king and barons. Still, we ought to keep in mind that the double function of the king put a severe strain on him, for in his theocratic function he was free and unhampered, could do as it pleased him. And the Roman law adage "What pleases the prince has the force of law" could so easily be invoked. Accordingly, many are the examples in which the king tried to minimize the obligations which the feudal function had put on him. Whether the feudal or the theocratic side of kingship prevailed in the end depended on the concrete situation and circumstances, that is, whether the theocratic king was skillful enough to circumvent his feudal obligations or whether the direct vassals of the king, his feudal tenants-in-chief, were vigilant enough in asserting their feudal rights, whether they had, in other words, become aware of the theocratic king's attempts to erode the rights which the feudal contract itself gave them. In any case there can be little doubt that the road from an unfettered theocratic *point d'appui* leading to constitutionalism was bloodstained and signposted by revolution and that the road from the feudal *point d'appui* leading to constitutionalism and, hence, to the constitutional fixation of the individual's rights was characterized by debates, compromise, in a word, by evolution.

Historical scholarship has come to recognize that in the West the turn of the twelfth and thirteenth centuries formed the period in which the seeds for the future constitutional development as well as for the standing of the individual in society were sown. Certainly in England, it was in that period that some basic principles of a feudal government were put effectively into operation and the hitherto largely private character of feudal relations became a province of public law.[17] Quite unlike his very able and gifted contemporary adversary

---

[17] See also Mitteis, *Staat*, pp. 375f.

Philip Augustus of France, the King of England, John, attempted with inadequate means to make real some of the claims which the by then rather fashionable jurisprudential doctrines of the civilian jurists had set forth. In so doing, however, John proceeded so clumsily and so ineptly that he aroused a good deal of opposition in the ranks of those who were primarily affected by his governmental measures, namely the barons.[18] Their main grievance was not the misuse but the overuse of the king's monarchic powers.

It seems appropriate to underscore the extremely severe dilemma which faced the baronage. After all, John was the Lord's anointed; in his function as theocratic Ruler he was removed from the jurisdiction or power of his subjects. How, then, were they to restrain him? How were they to put fetters on him? As mere subjects of the king, the barons never could restrict his powers, nor did they ever try, because as subjects they had not given him any power and could not, therefore, take it away or modify it. Although they were subjects, the barons, it must be remembered, were also feudal vassals, and in this capacity their relationship to the king was of an entirely different order. Here indeed was the platform which made it possible—perhaps for the last time— to fetter the king in a way which their status as subjects did not allow them. The wings of the theocratic King John were clipped, and clipped they were by the provisions of a thoroughly feudal document which he in his capacity as theocratic king issued. I can do no better than quote the words of Sidney Painter concerning the double function of the king:

> It is extremely important to remember [Painter said] that John was king as well as feudal lord of England and that this distinction was fully understood by the men of his day.[19]

[18] For a recent account see J. C. Holt, *Magna Carta* (Cambridge, 1965), esp. pp. 105ff.

[19] Sidney Painter, *The Reign of King John* (Baltimore, 1949), pp. 326–27.

Of the many articles of Magna Carta, the thirty-ninth is of special concern to us here: it is no doubt of some interest to note that in its basic structure and substance it went back to a feudal law issued by the German king Conrad II in 1037, a law which the framers of Magna Carta found in the easily available *Liber Feudorum:*[20]

> No freeman shall be captured and imprisoned, or disseized, or outlawed, or exiled, or in any way harmed, except by a *lawful tribunal of his peers* and by the *law of the land.*[21]

[20] *Liber Feudorum* v. 1; *M.G.H., Const.* i. 90. 46. For other influences, notably the *Leges Anglorum,* see Ullmann, *Principles of Government,* p. 161, to which should be added the method of trial decreed by Henry II in 1174, *Gesta Henrici II,* ed. W. Stubbs (Rolls Series; London, 1867), I, lxxxff.

[21] I would like to emphasize again what really should be in no need of emphasis, that the wording of Article 39 makes it abundantly clear that the framers plainly distinguished between the meanings of *vel* and *aut* in this article. It is not frequently recognized that they employ *aut* when they indubitably mean *or* and that they use *vel* when they mean *and.* The latter is used for "capiatur vel imprisonetur" as well as for the "judicium parium suorum vel per legem terrae," while in all other instances they use *aut.* In the former the conjunctive nature emerges when due consideration is given to the simple fact that one cannot be imprisoned without first having been captured: the two actions are conjoined; and a similar consideration obtains for the second instance, because a lawfully composed tribunal (of peers) must apply some law (here "the law of the land")—the one can do nothing without the other. Contemporary legal records in England as well as chroniclers mean by *judicium* a trial, that is, legal proceedings. For some observations on this topic, see Ullmann, *Principles of Government,* pp. 162f. Mitteis, *Staat,* p. 367, n. 95, had already pointed out that the *judicium parium* and the *lex terrae* "keine echten Gegensätze sind" and that, therefore, the *vel* was not disjunctive. Good jurist as he was, Mitteis stressed (*ibid.*) that the *lex terrae* was "materielles Recht" and that it was not to be understood as procedural law: "Ueberhaupt ist die lex terrae nicht prozessual zu verstehen." See Charles H. McIlwain in *Columbia Law Review,* XIV (1914), 50: "The former prescribes the manner of application, the latter the law to be applied. They are complementary to each other, not alternatives"; Paul Vinogradoff, in *Magna Carta Commemoration Essays* (London, 1917), p. 85: "The struggle was waged to secure trial in properly constituted courts of justice and in accordance with established law." The interpretation of Article 39 by Holt, *Magna Carta,* pp. 226ff., is quite inadequate, because he is obviously unfamiliar with the basic jurisprudential problems. That the profound significance of this article did not strike him can cause no surprise. See also below, n. 32.

It is indubitably correct to say that this article initiated what came to be called the rule of law[22] and that it contained in embryonic form the principle of due process of law.[23] It gains additional significance because the law of the land was the basis of judgments to be issued by a properly constituted tribunal in the cases mentioned. I believe that for the first time we are here presented with what at a later age came to be called the common law of England. The grievance of the baronial party was precisely that John had set aside the obligations imposed on him by the feudal compact, the essence of which was consent and advice between the parts of the contract, the joint machinery, and had instead attempted to rule on the basis of his own will, the *voluntas principis*. This became particularly noticeable in the numerous disseizins, imprisonments, outlawries, and banishments, in other words, in just the very matters which Article 39 explicitly mentioned.

What the barons wished to see applied was not the king's law, which he had issued on his own, but the law of the land, which referred to that body of written and unwritten rules which had its roots in native feudalism and which derived its material ingredients from the implicit or explicit consent of both king and barons. The law of the land of Article 39 was the law common to the king (in his feudal capacity) and the feudal baronage. It was common because previously both king and tenants-in-chief had acted upon it, had in other words given their approval, their consent, to it. After all, it was the king's own justices who had largely administered and fixed that law.

The presence of consent (which in the overwhelming majority of cases was of course implicit) as the substantive

[22] See on this most recently Gottfried Dietze, *Magna Carta and Property* (Magna Carta Essays; Charlottesville, Va., 1965), esp. pp. 39–40, with copious literature.

[23] See Sidney Painter, *The Rise of the Feudal Monarchies* (Ithaca, repr. 1964), p. 70.

element in the incipient common law[24] is illustrated by the verdict of the barons at the Diet of Merton. As decisively as one might wish, they rejected the clerical plea for giving rights of inheritance to an illegitimately born son who, by the provision of Roman as well as of canon law, became automatically legitimized by virtue of the marriage of the parents. In rejecting this plea, the barons also gave their reasons: We do not want to change the law of England because this was approved and used (*approbata et usitata*). The law to which they referred was in actual fact a feudal law embodied in the *Liber Feudorum*.[25] This kind of law, common to the king (in his feudal function) and the most important section of the populace, the baronage, was to be the third great system of law in medieval Europe: next to Roman, next to canon law, there was the common law; and this common law was an effective barrier to the influx of Roman law into England, an effective barrier above all to the full deployment of the descending theme of government and law which was so intimately connected with contemporary Roman law doctrines. Both Roman and canon law had one and the same basis: the *voluntas principis*, while the developing common law had as its substance the joint effort, the joint consultation, in other words, the co-operation and teamwork and consent of both parties to the feudal contract. As a native law, the common law was to have all the appurtenances of its feudal progenitor—flexibility, adjustability, resilience, and ease of accomodation to all sorts of new conditions, precisely because ultimately it went back to the individual and personal contract between lord and vassal.

In all these considerations the essential point is that in

[24] It is here that the customary law displayed its effects within the feudal sphere. For customary law see above and see also Painter, *Feudalism and Liberty*, p. 249: "A lord could never be an arbitrary, absolute ruler—he was bound by the contract, by the customs forged in his court. He had no power over the vassal other than that given him by custom."
[25] *Liber Feudorum* ii. 26. 11.

Article 39 of the original charter we find certain individual rights protected by the law, and that law was nothing else than what later was termed the common law, the offspring of feudal law. It goes beyond human ingenuity to devise a scheme of the subject's rights within the descending theme and to devise a protection of the subject's rights; for within the descending theme of government, the subject, precisely because he was a subject, had no other rights than those which were conferred upon him. The law could be changed by one stroke of the pen by the theocratic monarch. What is often overlooked in the assessment of the charter, therefore, is that it had a stipulation which shows rather clearly how consistent the framers were: the statement in Article 17 that common pleas no longer followed the king demonstrates, I think, clearly enough that the law and its administration were to be separated from the king's court still sitting *coram rege:* it is a statement which testifies to the independence of the law from the physical environs of the king himself. The wisdom of the common law lay precisely in this—that it still left to the king a number of functions, later to be called prerogatives, which he had by virtue of his theocratic functions. The Great Charter did not do away with the theocratic king at all, but it clipped his wings by bringing to bear upon him ancient feudal practice.

The explicit legal existence and, consequently, the protection of specifically individual rights seem sufficient evidence that feudal law and feudal practice itself had brought about the awareness of certain fundamental rights of the individual, rights, that is to say, which by the early thirteenth century could have grown on no ground other than the feudal one. There is as yet no indication whatsoever that these rights were the effluence of a divine law or of a natural law; these rights had not been conceded, had not been granted, had not been derived from superior authority, but had gradually emerged as rights in the public sphere. Although originally the feudal contract had been a private compact, by virtue of the king's having become a party to the feudal compact, the compact ceased to be a merely private one and became a constituent part of kingly, public government itself. In a passage which has not yet been properly appreciated, Sidney Painter said:

> The feudal concept of a system of law that governed the relations between lords and vassals was carried over into the realm of non-feudal political relationships.[26]

Indeed, these rights of the individual in Article 39 therefore became part of the public law, because Magna Carta itself constituted and was intended to constitute public law issued by the king with the counsel and advice of his barons. It is worthwhile to bear in mind this gradual, almost imperceptible transition of private to public law, effected in the feudal sphere and, above all, within the feudal-royal government. In brief, the individual's safety, freedom, and property were declared inviolate, were removed from arbitrary interference—in a thoroughly feudal document. This result could never have come about within the precincts of the theocratic-descending form of government.[27]

How decisive a role the contents of Article 39 of Magna Carta played in the preliminary discussions, negotiations, and debates which eventually led to the final product can be gathered convincingly from the fact that it was the substance of this article which formed the very first entry in the preparatory draft agreement between King John and the barons. A text of this draft or an *aide-mémoire* or a minute is in the *Trésor des chartes,* in which the French kings preserved all records of interest to their government.

---

[26] Painter, *King John,* p. 327.

[27] In his all too brief discussion of Article 39, Painter (*Feudalism and Liberty,* p. 248) nevertheless put his finger on the vital point: "New rights were added as changing conditions made them needful. Thus the basic feudal idea has remained one of the fundamental political principles of Anglo-American peoples."

Here in this text[28] the first "concession" of John was that
he would not capture any man without trial:

> Concedit rex Johannes quod non capiat hominem absque
> judicio.

It seems superfluous to comment upon the significance of the
order of the entry. In the document which informs us of the
early steps eventually leading to the issue of the charter,
there figure in the first place and in still somewhat embryonic
form the substance and contents of Article 39. It is the very
first item and heads all other "concessions" and promises by
the king—"it is the most fundamental of all baronial demands."[29] Above all, what the barons were concerned with
was legal security of at least the freeman, was *Rechtssicher-
heit,* was the elimination of arbitrariness in government. This
was a great step forward in the perennial quest for protecting
the individual from government interference.[30] The place
which the persons directly involved in drafting a settlement
assign to a particular piece symptomatically reflects their own
assessment of the question settled.

One should beware, however, of projecting later conceptions into this Article 39 of Magna Carta. Above all, it
contains little that may be called democratic, for the court
or tribunal envisaged was composed of peers, which seems

[28] Alexandre Teulet, *Layettes du Trésor des Chartes* (Paris, 1863), I,
423, no. 1153.

[29] Painter, *King John,* p. 315. He also considered "that it took a more
than feudal mind to place this provision ahead of those that were purely
feudal in scope."

[30] For the dating of this text, see F. Maurice Powicke, *Stephen
Langton* (Oxford, 1928), p. 119 (autumn 1213 to summer 1214); as
regards the character of the text, see Charles Petit-Dutaillis, *Studies and
Notes supplementary to Stubbs' Constitutional History,* trans. W. E.
Rhodes (Manchester, 1908), pp. 121ff.; see also Charles Petit-Dutaillis,
L'essor des états d'occident (2d ed.; Paris, 1944), pp. 169–70; further,
Mitteis, *Staat,* p. 365, n. 92; Barnaby Keeney, *Judgment by Peers* (Cam-
bridge, Mass., 1949), p. 152, n. 8; Painter, *King John,* pp. 311ff.;
Christopher R. Cheney, "The eve of Magna Carta," *Bulletin of the John
Rylands Library,* XXXVIII (1956), 331, n. 1; Holt, *Magna Carta,*
pp. 296ff. (without offering any new point of view).

a rather clear indication that thinking in terms of an estate was still the dominant theme in this context. Magna Carta is firmly linked with the past; the *Leges Henrici* of a century earlier had stated, "Everybody must be judged by his peers."[31] One might go even further and say that the division of society into its estates, with its clear implications of the "higher" and "lower" ranking orders of estates, was in fact given a new lease on life insofar as the practice in the feudal courts became a constitutional principle.[32] The ability to sit in a court trying an individual depended, therefore, upon one's membership in a particular estate or rank within an estate. In a roundabout way one returns again to the old principle that the higher cannot be judged by the lower.[33]

Within this context Article 14 of the Great Charter demands a few words. This article was, so to speak, an ordinance which in detail implemented the general statute of Article 12, according to which scutage could be levied only "by the common counsel of my realm." But Article 14 states that decisions should also be binding upon those who, though summoned, had not appeared at a meeting. We need not go into the question of how only a minority of those who had

---

[31] Liebermann, *Die Gesetze der Angelsachsen*, I, 564 (31. 7 and 33. 1).

[32] For some details see Keeney, *Judgment by Peers*, pp. 58ff. Keeney's view on the meaning of *freeman* (pp. 57f.) seems to me sensible and plausible. See also Bloch, *Feudal Society*, pp. 359, 368ff.; and Dawson, *Lay Judges*, p. 289, who assessed the principle of trial by peers correctly when he stated that "it moves into recorded history in the context of feudal relationships. It was first clearly phrased as the right of an individual vassal to be judged by his fellow vassals." The term *judicium* did not mean, in contemporary juristic language, judgment, but tribunal, court, trial proceedings. See my remarks in *Principles of Government*, p. 163, n. 1. The numerous complaints against John, which maintained that he had proceeded *sine judicio*, did not mean that he had proceeded "without judgment," but "without lawful trial."

[33] This was indeed what a contemporary document had: see the passage in Pollock and Maitland, *English Law* (2d ed.; Cambridge, 1926), I, 173, n. 3. See also above, p. 15, and *Leges Henrici* 5.8 (in Liebermann, *Die Gesetze der Angelsachsen*, I, 549).

been summoned and had appeared could make decisions binding upon the majority, which had not come to the meeting; nor do we need to inquire into the principle of representation in this article. All that it is necessary to say is that the envisaged procedure was wholly alien to feudal law and feudal conceptions—though it was a familiar one in the current canon law—which still operated on the basis of the individual contract, with the individual voting and consenting. It causes no surprise that this article was excised from all subsequent reissues of Magna Carta, because it contained a principle that could not be squared with fundamental feudal ideas.[34]

In the thirteenth century the common law of which we have the first heraldings in the Great Charter was still a very tender plant which could grow and develop only if cultivated properly. One thing is clear: despite repeated efforts by the king in the thirteenth century to repossess himself of unfettered theocratic functions, both reality and the precedent of the Great Charter proved themselves too strong to be overcome. The subsequent development of the common law is so intimately connected with the constitutional development that they are the same coin, only seen from different angles. One must not forget that the common law was still only the law that united the king (in his feudal capacity) and the baronage and that there remained large enclaves which were untouched by the common law.[35] It is worth remembering, however, that in the course of the

[34] The manner of raising scutage (Article 12) was in the re-issue of 1217, Article 44, to be handled according to the custom prevailing at the time of Henry II.

[35] This fact Magna Carta itself also seems to have recognized and can be found throughout thirteenth-century England, when there was, on certain points, a "contrast between the common law and the custom of the country side" (Homans, *English Villagers*, p. 165). By no means did all manorial customs comply with the common law. The Kentish laws were another example; see for this and other instances Charles H. McIlwain, "Magna Carta and the common law," in *Magna Carta Commemoration Essays*, p. 135.

constitutional development the greater the sections of the populace were which became constitutionally operational, the more the common law spread its wings, the more it became common to the king and the other emancipated estates of the realm.

The significance of this evolution seems clear enough. Without grand speculations, the feudal compact itself furnished a sufficiently strong base from which a later theory of individual rights and duties could, as it did, emerge. This individual relationship was a reciprocal relationship based upon the feudal contract, which was to display its influence far beyond feudalism, far beyond the constitution, and was to radiate into all departments of social and public life. One might indeed go as far as to say that the slowly emerging constitution was the consequence of the rights which feudal practice had attributed to the individual. All this stands, of course, in somewhat somber contrast to the unrealistic view which contemporary doctrine had taken of the individual as a mere recipient of orders and laws.

Moreover, because the law was the result of a joint effort, even the king could be held to it, could in other words be forced to keep the law by those with whom he had *made* it. This indeed is the significance of the coronation promises which Edward II in 1308 had to take: now the community of the realm—the constitutional offspring of the feudal community—had the right to enforce the law against the king, because he had given his consent to the law which he could not unilaterally change, as Bracton nearly two generations before had said.[36] It seems evident that this evolution had provided in the Middle Ages a platform on which the essential element of the law-creative process, namely consent, could be practically realized. Mere subjects of the king could

[36] About the differences between the first three clauses and the fourth clause of Edward II's coronation promises, see Ullmann, *Principles of Government*, pp. 185ff.

never hope, by legitimate means, to enforce the law against the king. The law was *given* to them, not made by them. But law-making contained as an essential ingredient the consent of those to whom the law was to apply. It is at this juncture that the ancient (but, within the descending framework of government, forgotten) *consensus utentium* received its concrete application and precision. Paradoxically one might say that the Ciceronian axiom became revived and applied by a wholly un-Ciceronian institution, by feudalism. For the consent of those to whom the law was to apply was the very backbone of parliament, even if only by construction, and was to lead to the invocation of the (misunderstood) Roman law passage "What touches all must be approved by all,"[37] so that with the ever widening circle of those claiming to be entitled to give their consent and assent to the law, the law became common to all.[38]

How potently the ground had been prepared for the reception of some seemingly radical views can easily be proved by a few statements made in the fourteenth century. For instance, on the occasion of Edward III's coronation, in 1327, a medal was struck which had as its inscription *Voluntas populi dat jura*—the will of the people gives law;[39] or Chief Justice Thorpe, in the same reign, said: Parliament represents the body of all the realm; or the statement was made that "the law of the land is made in parliament by the king and the spiritual and temporal lords and the whole community of the realm." The point here is that the new

[37] About this see Herbert F. Jolowicz, "The stone which the builders rejected," *South African Law Review*, VIII (1956), 73ff.

[38] See the admirable pages of McIlwain, in *Magna Carta Commemoration Essays*, pp. 142ff. The further pursuit of these ideas belongs to constitutional history, especially the idea of representation. "Only gradually did the theory arise that the whole of England was constructively in parliament; that they were all assumed to be there consenting to what parliament did. The theory of representation was complete in the fourteenth century," *ibid.*, p. 144; see also *ibid.*, p. 169.

[39] Quoted from Michael J. Wilks, *The Problem of Sovereignty in the Later Middle Ages* (Cambridge, 1963,) p. 190, n. 2.

ascending principles of government, so much broadcast at this very time on the Continent, could and did find an easy ingress into the feudally soaked ground in England and this without the reverberations which such principles otherwise would have caused. The practical significance of this preparation was that it could serve as a base for the doctrinal transmutation of the subject into a citizen. The feudal community—amorphous indeed, ill-defined and unwieldy—came to be taken as the *populus* whose constituent members were the individuals themselves as citizens with their own rights and duties. It would take me too far afield if in this context I were to go into a detailed analysis of the invocation of the pure Roman law and its so-called *lex regia,* but it may be said with confidence that feudal practice and feudal conceptions, assuredly unwittingly, gave reality and meaning to the views expressed in Ulpian's statement. One thing is clear and stands out: it was on the stony soil of feudal conceptions that the practice emerged which ascribed certain rights to the members of the feudal community, rights which they had not as a result of the king's good will, his grace or favor, but which they had by virtue of the simple fact that they were members of the feudal community. Only fundamental feudal conceptions could give rise to the protection, by law, of the rights enumerated in the Great Charter; this could never, as history has proved, be achieved within the sphere of a theocratic form of government. Allow me to quote a statement by one of America's outstanding medievalists, happily still among us:

> Feudalism is the stage through which English institutions passed and were still passing at the time when the common law was forming and the functions of parliament developing, and the participation of the "estates" in "legislation" can no more be understood without taking this into account than can the existence of these estates themselves.[40]

[40] McIlwain, in *Magna Carta Commemoration Essays,* p. 153.

I have said that the rights of the individual (or at least
of the freeman) as enumerated in Article 39 of the Great
Charter became, through being embodied in this Charter,
part of the public law, which was here none other than
feudal law and which signified nothing less than the subjection of the king to the law. What Magna Carta had
achieved was indubitably also the aim of a number of
theoreticians, and I think one can go as far as to say that
throughout the Middle Ages efforts were made to bind the
Ruler to the law and subject him to it. That the descending
thesis of government and law provided little encouragement
in this direction should have become clear by now. Nevertheless, there was always the one or the other voice which, in
order to achieve this subjection of the Ruler to the law,
maintained that there was a *pactum* or a *pactio*, in other
words, a contract between Ruler and subjects.[41] This design
was no doubt an ill-fitting device, because it militated against
the very core and substance of the theocratic-descending
thesis of government, which did not deviate from the view
that the subjects were entrusted or committed to the king by
divinity.[42] The significance of these efforts to envisage a contract lies in this—that, despite their adherence to the
descending theme, some writers felt uneasy about the unrestricted power of the Ruler and looked for a handle to
restrict him. That handle was believed to lie in the alleged
contract between him and his subjects. Another means which
was intended to produce some subjection of the king to his

[41] See, for example, Rufinus in the twelfth century, *De bono pacis*
ii. 9 (*Patr. Lat.* cl. 1617): "When the king is instituted, he enters into
a tacit agreement [*pactio quaedam tacita*] with the people, with a view to
ruling the people in a humane manner. . . ." Before him Manegold of
Lautenbach (in *M.G.H., Libelli de Lite* i. 365) held similarly that "the
people had a right to free itself from the rule and subjection of the king,
because it was clear that it was he who had first broken the contract
(*pactum*) by which he was made king." See also Engelbert of Admont
(in the thirteenth century), in his *De Ortu Romani Imperii* cap. 2
(*pactum subjectionis* between Ruler and people).

[42] See also above, p. 18.

subjects was the invocation of the panacea provided by natural law. It was precisely in this context that a significant shift in the view of the Ruler's governing power emerged.

It is not yet fully recognized that the prevalence of feudal law and feudal conception also provided the theoreticians of the law, mainly the Roman lawyers, with a platform that enabled them to restrict the Ruler's plenitude of power. It was increasingly maintained that, despite his legislative omnipotence, that is, despite his plenitude of power, he could not deprive a vassal of his fief unless the latter were convicted, before his peers, of a felony. This point of view would not be worth mentioning were it not that the feudal customs upon which it was based were presented as falling within the category of natural law, and every Ruler was said to be bound by the natural law.[43] The significance of

[43] As far as I can ascertain, the problem was first clearly perceived by the thirteenth-century jurist Guido de Suzaria as reported by Cynus. See the latter's report, *Commentaria ad Codicem* i. 14.3 (Digna vox) (ed. Frankfurt, 1586), fol. 26ra, no. 7: "Sciendum quod Guido de Suzaria formavit hic quaestionem, utrum si imperator ineat aliqua pacta cum aliqua civitate vel barone, teneatur ea observare tam ipse quam eius successor . . . naturalia jura suadent pacta servari et fides etiam hostibus est servanda. . . ." Baldus, *In usus feudorum commentaria* (Lyons, 1585) i. De feudo guardiae. cap. Notandum. fol. 8v. no. 2: The Ruler cannot divest a vassal "quia bonae et naturales consuetudines ligant principem, quia potentius est jus naturale quam principatus"; *ibid.*, fol. 18v: "Pone, quod imperator vel rex Francorum creat aliquem ducem et investit eum de ducatu vel marchionem et investit eum de marchionatu . . . numquid protest pro libito disvestire eum? Respondeo, quod non, sed demum propter convictam culpam vel feloniam. Adde, quod nec successores in imperio vel regno possent. . . . Nec obstat quod imperator habeat plenitudinem potestatis, quia verum est quod Deus subiecit ei leges, sed non subiecit ei contractus, ex quibus obligatus est." Further, Baldus *Codex* vi. 58. Authentica "Omnes peregrini." fol. 196r. no. 7: no deprivation of a fief "nisi prius per pares judicentur indigni." See further Ludovicus Romanus Pontanus *Consilia* (ed. Lyons, 1586) consil. 352. fol. 184v. no. 24, and *Tractatus Universi Iuris* xi–1. fol. 24v. no. 9: "Consuetudo feudorum censetur jus naturale." It is high time that this whole cluster of problems and ideas is properly investigated. It should perhaps also be pointed out that in the English *Leges Henrici* of the early twelfth century there is a statement which has some resemblance to the views expressed by these latter jurists: 49. 5a (in Liebermann, *Die Gesetze der Angelsachsen,* I, 472): "Pactum legem vincit"; Glanville had: "Conventio legem vincit," *ibid.*, n. i

this theoretical development was that pure jurisprudential doctrine in regard to the Ruler's relation to his subjects was considerably modified, and modified it was through the influence of the feudal law and customs, now even appearing as an issue of the natural law. In other words, the feudal standpoint came to be incorporated in the doctrine of the Ruler's power, which, for practical and theoretical purposes, found in the "naturalized" feudal law a severe barrier. Moreover, contractual arrangements entered into by the Ruler were also binding upon his successors, so that the sovereignty of the Ruler became affected quite seriously by this doctrine. Perhaps nothing reveals better the juristic embarrassment of the great jurist Baldus than the argument employed by him: God, he said, had subjected the laws to the Ruler's power, but not contracts made by him—a standpoint which, from the juristic angle, is difficult to reconcile. I think it is not too precipitate to say that the infusion of a positive and concrete contractual element into pure juristic doctrine might well be considered a preparatory step toward the full contract theory of a later age, and it was a step which so potently and obviously was suggested by feudal arrangements. There is, then, considerable justification, I think, in Marc Bloch's statement, "The clearest legacy of feudalism to modern societies is the emphasis placed upon the notion of the political contract."[44]

It does not seem too difficult to understand why the English legal and political scene provided such healthy and fertile ground for the practical and enduring utilization of feudal ideas. This is especially important for my topic, because—however paradoxical it may sound—these feudal ideas also exercised great equalizing influence. After the Conquest there was nobody who did not hold from someone else, or if from no one else, then he held from the king. The significance of this feature is that there were not two

[44] *Theories of Society,* p. 386.

(or more) kinds of subjects, because all were in one way or another vassals. Feudal law, therefore, was applicable to all conditions of man in England—"of all European countries England was the most perfectly feudalized"—and through its equalizing effects it prevented, above all, the emergence of a caste: it served for the tenant by knight service no less than for the tenant in socage or for the agricultural classes.[45]

This strongly pronounced equalizing effect of the feudal law—not in a social, but in a legal sense—accounts for the often observed popular features of the early growing common law, which indeed incorporated the consent of those to whom it applied, even if this consent was assuredly one of construction. This sturdily growing common law was not a law that was forged in the workshops of the great jurisconsults in the universities. It was not a law that exhibited much legal theorizing, that could hardly be compared with the gleaming jurisprudential systems and their subtle refinements as propounded by the professional jurists. It was, if I may use the term, a jurisprudence of actualities and was founded, above all, on common consent.[46] This incipient common law was not, as Roman law certainly was, a historic anachronism; the common law was not the attempt to distill pure ecclesiastical doctrine or theological dogmas into the law, as instanced by canon law. The common law was, in the most literal sense, a living law made by the men who stood with both feet firmly and squarely on the ground. Although it was a tender plant in the thirteenth century, it was, nonetheless, a rather sturdy one. One can see quite easily how steadily this body of law developed when one looks at the Year Books. In many ways the Year Books are a unique English invention, possibly even prompted by the new kind of law, but in any case they are first-class witnesses

[45] Frederic W. Maitland, *Constitutional History* (Cambridge, 1926), pp. 156f., where the quotation in the text will also be found.
[46] R. L. Fowler in *Columbia Law Review*, XIII (1913), 596, 603.

to the growth of the common law, for in them we see in a vivid manner how the individual items of the law came to be hammered out in concrete cases. The Year Books are photographic reproductions or slow-motion pictures of the process of the making of the law. Having detached itself, in course of time, from its progenitor and having become, so to speak, adult, the common law came to embody its own inherent force, its own dynamic principles; in a word, it became an authority of its own.

Administration of justice is always the linchpin of government, and nowhere is this more true than in medieval England, for government and law were there—as everywhere else—the two sides of the same coin. By administering the law, it is developed, refined, and clarified. It is not always properly appreciated that the handling of legal business in thirteenth- and fourteenth-century England was very largely in the hands of the unpaid amateur, of the non-professional: it was the laymember of the (feudal) community at large who was harnessed to the administration of the law. Large numbers of the local gentry were pressed into service to preside at trials, to receive the verdicts of juries, to pronounce judgment; the Henrician possessory assizes were handled by justices who were knights and who had received special commissions;[47] in the county courts it was the sheriff and the suitors who arrived at the judgment; "the county court spoke as a body, for the county as a whole. . . . It *was* the country personified."[48] Similar observations can be made about the Hundred Court, the jurisdiction of which affected the local community.

[47] We should observe that Article 18 of Magna Carta envisaged the association of four knights of the shire with the quarterly circuits held by the two justices, which seems to be the acknowledgment of lay participation in dealing with the assizes. Though this article was later modified, it nevertheless announced an important principle; see also Pollock and Maitland, *English Law*, I, 200–1.

[48] Dawson, *Lay Judges*, p. 179, also for the substance of this paragraph. For some general observations see, further, G. Sawer, *Law in Society* (Oxford, 1965), pp. 76ff., 94–95.

Nor should one forget that the legal business thus transacted touched the very life of ordinary men and women, moved, in other words, very near to the grass roots of contemporary society. That this harnessing of the populace to the administration of law was highly conducive to local government is obvious, but is of no immediate interest to me here; what is of interest is that close association with the law did not produce the sentiment so frequently observed in other societies, that is, of the law as something standing aside and apart from the people itself. What is further significant is that the central courts did not interfere in the trials of the lower courts unless the latter broke procedural rules, in which case a writ *De falso judicio* could be entered.[49] One might well advance the view that it was on the rugged and rough ground of feudalism that society achieved a degree of integration which was hardly paralleled in any other society, for the active participation of large parts of society in administering and thereby practically shaping the law was merely another way of taking part in government itself: the application, administration, adjustment of the law was in the hands of many individuals whom it would have been anomalous to refer to as *idiotae*.[50] Moreover, this participation presupposed a sense of responsibility, a sense of social consciousness, and a sense of social duty on the part of the individuals —all of which would be hard to match in societies in which the descending theme of government was applied. In more than one sense one can say that the law was common and that this common law consequently produced a homogeneous and integrated society through manipulation by a thoroughly feudalized community. Both the law and the society were earth-bound, far removed from all doctrinal speculation, and because they were earth-bound, they of necessity and in a practical manner respected certain rights of the individual,

[49] Very rarely was there interference in regard to substantive law; Dawson, *Lay Judges*, pp. 275–76.
[50] See above, p. 62.

because all individuals in one way or another were engaged
in the same process.

Moreover, on the occasion of the judge's *iter* (his eyre)
it was the county (or county court) which acted in some
quasi-corporate capacity,[51] by which it testified to customs,
to the position of towns, to the manner of proving certain
facts, and the like. Towns, too, were present before the king's
judges, and they spoke through their representatives—indeed, without grand theories representative government as
a matter of practice manifested itself in these proceedings
before the common law administrators.[52] This law was man-
made; a large part of the population was involved in these
proceedings. Another point which one must never forget in
these considerations is that the language was English, not the
learned Latin, but the language of the ordinary individuals.
(I refer of course to the oral pleadings and debates.) On the
other hand, we have not a single case reported from the
Roman curia or the imperial court. When later at Avignon
the papal judicial Rota did issue records, they looked like
learned treatises in canon law, from which all the pulsating
life, all the cut and thrust of healthy argument, had been
driven out. Unlike them the common law showed vigorous
life in its early stages, and it showed it because ordinary
mankind had taken part in its making. At all times law is a
mirror of a particular society, and the plea-rolls and Year
Books reflect that feudal society extremely well: they are
much more reliable witnesses of social and cultural history
than scholarly tracts. In these mirrors the common lawyer
of the thirteenth century is revealed as a very important
instrument in preparing the ground for the adoption of the
proper ascending theme of government. In one of his memo-
rable passages Maitland once said that this common lawyer
"mediated between the abstract Latin logic of the schoolmen

[51] Frederic W. Maitland, *Pleas of the Crown, Gloucestershire* (London,
1884), p. xxiv.
[52] *Ibid.*, p. xxv.

and the concrete needs and homely talk of gross, unschooled mankind. Law was the point where life and logic met."[53]

For in the Year Books one can witness the cut and thrust of legal argument, the judge's reticence in accepting novel arguments, and above all, the juristic discussion and precedential character of decisions. It is frequently forgotten that the Year Books contain the best proof of the parentage of the common law, for they tell us that royal letters were challenged and even declared contrary to the law—inevitably one sees the contrast between this kind of law and government with its opposite number, where to challenge the validity of a royal statement was tantamount to denying the basis of royal power. As a matter of fact, the law courts, the workings of which are so vividly portrayed in the Year Books, were concerned with this very problem of the king's alleged plenitude of power, because he was said to be on the same level as the pope, "who can do everything" ("papa omnia potest") and, hence, also change the law by unilateral declaration. That the courts did not uphold this doctrine we know from the Year Books.[54] It was through this medium that later generations—one has but to think of Cooke— came to know the law, but perhaps more important is the observation that the Year Books show us the role of the common law as a vehicle shaping what without fear of gainsaying may be held as the constitutional development itself. Many years ago Paul Vinogradoff made a statement which is particularly apt to bring into relief the role of the common law as far as my topic is concerned:

> The Law Courts [he said in his Creighton Lecture] in framing rights and remedies for the citizens led to habits of minds which were bound to be applied to the relations between Ruler and subjects.[55]

[53] Frederic W. Maitland, *Year-Books* (Selden Soc., 1903), I, xxxvii.
[54] See Paul Vinogradoff, "Constitutional History and the Year Books," *Law Quarterly Review*, XXIX (1913), 282.
[55] *Ibid.*, p. 284.

The individual could obtain redress for wrongs and uphold his rights within the law, and did not receive these rights, as in the other governmental system, as a matter of royal grace.

It may very well be that a government that was based on feudal conceptions and consequently had to operate within the law showed none of the gleaming appurtenances which characterized the working of a theocratic form of government. This kind of government may well appear chromium-plated, streamlined, air-conditioned, and highly efficient. A feudal government, drawing its strength from the rugged but highly fertile native soil, was no doubt slow; its machinery was creaking and heavy and cumbersome, and it had to work with the consent and counsel of unlearned, if not unlettered, magnates—but from the historical point of view it supplied the basis of a constitutional development and of the thesis of the individual's rights. Above all, it exercised influence far beyond the Middle Ages and also beyond the confines of the constitution itself, while the descending form of government atrophied into the servile *Beamtenstaat* or *Obrigkeitsstaat*. The legacy of feudal conceptions and feudal law to later generations seems to me an incontrovertible fact, because they stressed the reciprocity of individual obligations and, therefore, of individual rights. An important part of this legacy of feudal conceptions and arrangements was respect for the law, because in the final resort all strata of feudal society were involved in making, applying, and adjusting the law: it was not regarded as something alien or imposed, but was the feudal members' own. Respect for the law, a result of a generations-long process, appears to me particularly marked in societies with a strong feudal past. Because there was consent, through the machinery of taking part in making and applying the law, the idea of obedience to the law by the individual assumed a complexion in these societies somewhat different from that in those societies where the law was "given."

It is, nonetheless, instructive to reflect, just for one moment, upon the effects which the replacement of a lay element by a professional body of trained administrators and jurists, especially in the judiciary, had upon society. This kind of reflection may also be conducive to a better understanding of the different political and constitutional developments in the various countries. It is not yet generally recognized that where the theocratic-descending thesis of government and law predominated, such as in France and Germany, attempts were made to bring the trained professional man to the fore, that is, not to leave the administration of justice in the hands of the people, in the hands of the untrained "amateur," as was so overwhelmingly the case in medieval England. Simultaneously the canonical inquisitorial mode of procedure was applied. Both these features, professionalism and mode of inquiry, had enduring influence upon the complexion of society. In the thirteenth century a supply of trained professional jurists could be secured fairly easily, because the universities provided them abundantly. In the universities there was training in the law and its principles, a fact which meant that the judicial officers appointed by the government applied the Roman-canonical axioms in practice. This Roman-canonical jurisprudence was highly intricate, with the consequence that the administration of justice came to be beyond the competence of the laymen.

The further consequence was that society was gradually evolving a different complexion altogether, since the most pronounced features connected with the administration of justice by laymen were no longer observable, that is, the idea of representation, promotion of local government, and so forth.[56] These professional government officers represented no community and were not responsible to anyone but the

---

[56] See above, p. 87. The absence of local government and the lack of any manifestation of a local public spirit on the Continent has often been remarked upon and bewailed, but an historical explanation is rarely to be found.

king.[57] This juristic professionalism produced, of course, important political and social consequences and implications in both France and Germany: its adoption accounted also for the social no less than for the purely legal influence of Roman and canon law in both countries. This is only another way of saying that both the society and the individual assumed a complexion fundamentally different from that of, say, feudal England, in which this Roman-canonical influence was so conspicuously absent. Because a governmental or public officer had received his power (his *imperium*, to use technical language) from superior authority, he himself was superior to ordinary man, who had not thus been distinguished. There was a direct causal link between the adoption of administrative professionalism resulting in officialdom and the prevalance of the theocratic-descending form of government.[58] The supply of professionally trained jurists by the universities provided the theocratically orientated governments with rather effective means to shape the society in their charge—with consequences far beyond the limited judicial and governmental issues. It is assuredly no coincidence that in the feudally soaked English ground the two universities played a considerably smaller role in governmental matters than the Inns of Court in London, in which the native common law formed the exclusive educational framework.[59] On this point it may be worthwhile to quote

[57] See Dawson, *Lay Judges*, pp. 60, 68, 87, 300.

[58] This raised status of public officers may also furnish an explanation for the feature observable in most continental criminal codes, according to which conduct which does not constitute a criminal offence when committed against a private person becomes so if committed against an officer. The term *officer* is so widely drawn that it includes foresters, highway patrolmen, railway guards, customs officers, servants of municipal corporations, firebrigade employees, etc. The criterion in all these cases is that the officer must have received a commission from some *Obrigkeit*. See also, for the *droit administratif*, below, p. 94.

[59] See Samuel E. Thorne, "The early history of the Inns of Court," *Graya* (1959), pp. 79–96. On the other hand, the common law could hardly be fitted into the curriculum of the law faculties in the two universities. It seems that William Blackstone was, at Oxford in 1758, the

the observation of Maitland:

> Let us notice [he said in his Rede Lecture at Cambridge] one difference which, if I am not mistaken, marked off England from the rest of the world. Medieval England had schools of national law.[60]

It was not jurists learned *in utroque jure,* but the practitioners "graduating" from the Inns of Court who knew no other legal system but the English common law and who staffed the royal courts.[61]

It is indeed not difficult to understand the readiness with which theocratic governments adopted the professionalism of the judicial officers. The government thereby gave concrete expression to its own underlying governmental ideas and laid the application of its own law into the hands of its servants. That a theocratic government—based as it so largely was upon the faith of the subjects—was particularly anxious to detect any movement and to eradicate the forces which somehow might threaten the basis of the theocratic Ruler is self-evident: one has but to refer to Louis IX of France, who in the first half of the thirteenth century adopted the principles of the inquisition to combat the heretics, thereby doing away with the ancient accusatorial principles of criminal procedure.[62] The adoption of these measures was, so to speak, if not dictated, at any rate suggested by the very ideology upon which a theocratic form of government rested. Officers thus armed with the full power and backing of the government carried the royal

---

first to lecture *ex professo* on the English law itself. It should be noted that in the seventies of the fourteenth century John Wycliffe already advocated the study of the English (common) law at the universities in preference to the Roman civil (and canon) law; see his *Select English Works,* ed. Thomas Arnold (Oxford, 1871), III, 326.

[60] See Frederic W. Maitland, *Selected Historical Essays,* ed. Helen M. Cam (Cambridge, 1957), p. 144.

[61] See William S. Holdsworth, *Sources and Literature of English Law* (Oxford, repr. 1952), p. 30.

[62] See above, p. 37.

volonté to the farthest corners of the kingdom. All this would
not be worth mentioning were it not that the machinery of
government came to rely more and more upon the professional "civil servant" in virtually all spheres of interest to
the government itself. The growth of the "civil service"
within the precincts of the descending forms of government
is a symptom which is not yet fully appreciated.[63] Not only
is this growth a large part of the reason that local government on the Continent—government characterized by the
active participation of the local, knowledgeable amateurs—
had never developed, but it is also a large part of the feature
which is equally characteristic of this manifestly applied
descending thesis, namely the special protection which government officers in the continental system enjoyed, a protection afforded to them by the provisions of a special code of
law which has become known as the *droit administratif*.

The significance of this code of law lies in this—that a
very sharp cleavage is drawn between the government offi-
cials and the ordinary citizen. The so-called Rule of Law does
not apply to the former, if he acts within his official capacity
and duty—it is a protection which puts the governmental
officers in many respects into a considerably more sheltered
position than that enjoyed by the ordinary citizen, who, by
the same token, is often exposed to the unchallengeable
plea of the public interest. It seems clear to me that, historically speaking, there has been, under a very thin veil of

[63] The far too frequently (especially on the Continent) encountered
identification of the State with the officers of the government and the
government itself may in the final resort go back to the ubiquitous and
easily recognizable body of government officers "who are the State." It
should be borne in mind, however, that similar conceptions prevailed in
the Hellenistic monarchy. See Ehrenberg, *Der Staat der Griechen*,
p. 191: "Der hellenistische Staat war eine Monarchie. Er bestand aus
dem König und seinen Untertanen, aber gerade deshalb war er kein
Staat als menschliche Gemeinschaft oder auch nur als gemeinsame
Angelegenheit [res publica]. Der Staat bedeutete die königliche Ver-
waltung, die öffentlichen Angelegenheiten des Königs, der König spricht
von 'unseren Angelegenheiten.' "

disguise, a continued emphasis on the concept of the office and the idea of public interest,[64] but there is also clear proof that it was the existence of the common law which prevented this very distinction between a specially protected government officer and the ordinary run of mankind. It does not seem too rash to state that it was the "undogmatic," unprofessional character of the early common law which, precisely because of its feudal parentage, could not and did not distinguish between government officers and others: before the law the former could not plead what was denied to the latter.

In the history of political ideas—at least as far as they relate to my topic—hardly any recognition is accorded, with some notable exceptions, to the potent influence which the predominance of feudal principles exercised upon the character of society. One must not assume that the feudal arrangements, with their social consequences, were confined to some strata of society only: on the contrary, they percolated, so to speak, to all sections and pervaded and impregnated them with basic feudal tenets, notably those of reciprocity, consent, and mutual rights and duties. These were not the result of doctrine or of the drawing of conclusions from First Principles, but were developed and applied on a purely practical plane. What seems to be in need of emphasis is that a feudal society showed definite signs of aversion to erecting elaborate doctrinal edifices and equally definite signs of an empirical approach to problems of social organization. The intellectual climate in thirteenth- and fourteenth-century England may well show features which distinguished it from contemporary continental scholarship. With particular force can this observation be made in regard to the study of law at contemporary Oxford and Cambridge—their scholarly legal output was at best poor compared to that produced at the great law schools on the Continent. Jurisprudence was,

---

[64] See above, pp. 16, 36.

literally speaking, merely an academic discipline. Law as treated in these two universities was far less related to contemporary social exigencies and conditions than it was at the great sees of legal learning on the Continent. One might here speak of a stunting of the legal mind, because academic law (for all practical purposes, Roman and canon law) did not evoke much response in contemporary society. What mattered in feudal society was not speculation and abstract dogma, but earthiness and practicability.[65] It was this practical and empirical outlook which, without speculation, attributed to the individual certain rights which he had for no other reason than that he was a member of feudal society.

In general, one may well venture the opinion that it did not need particular acumen at a later stage to envisage feudally practiced rights and duties of a member of the feudal community as natural rights and duties of the individual citizen. I think it was no historic freak or coincidence that the English common law became in the seventeenth century the bulwark of the individual liberties against what might well be called the irrepressible monarchic aspirations of the kings, because that law was, in its genesis and application, a law that had grown on feudal soil since the twelfth century and embodied the element of consent. I feel certain that the development of a theory of basic civic rights in the feudally impregnated England was historically conditioned, and the Virginia Declaration of 1776 was no more and no less than a historically conditioned abstract manifesto epitomizing in succinct form the individual's rights, in the last resort deducible from thoroughly feudal documents and feudal practices. The pivotal point is that, through its becoming legalized, the feudal system had fostered the idea of individual freedoms which were protected by the law. It is not without interest to see that Dicey treats the doctrine

[65] Touching upon the problem of academic law, Sawer, *Law in Society*, pp. 119f., makes no distinction between feudal and non-feudal societies.

of individual freedom in the section entitled "The Rule of Law." No natural law theory, no considerations of a doctrinal character, could have exercised influence if the historic presuppositions had not been favorable. It would appear, from the historical point of view, wholly understandable why, say, Locke or, for that matter, Blackstone, propounded their theories in seventeenth- and eighteenth-century England: the historic presuppositions made a doctrinal elaboration of the individual's rights feasible—the natural law doctrines furnished the doctrinal *pièce justificative* for the centuries-old practice, itself having no more distinguished paternity than the feudal law, feudal justice, and feudal arrangements.

This recognition also has wider implications insofar as it may explain, at least partly, not only the divergent developments in those countries in which feudal conceptions played only an insignificant role, but also why it was in the Anglo-Saxon countries that the thesis of the individual's rights had struck such deep and virtually ineradicable roots. How necessary the factual, if not the ideological, preparation is can be easily demonstrated by the feverish upheaval that followed the declaration of the French Constituante in 1789 on the inalienability of human rights: the French ground had not in the past been cultivated for the reception of these enchanting doctrines which were, as yet, no more than mere philosophic and theoretical speculations. The influence of the antecedent ideology in France turned such panoplied assertions into powerful instruments of bloody and contagious revolution. It was all very well to lay down formally and solemnly in the written constitutions of the nineteenth century the rights of the individual; the practical effects, nevertheless, somewhat stood in inverse proportion to the intellectual efforts which demanded such constitutional fixations. The Russian Revolution of 1917, too, incontrovertibly proved how much revolutionary energy—fed and sustained by pure dogmatic speculation—could be released, when all historical precedents, tradition, and, above all, preparation were wanting. In those countries, however, in which feudal government and feudal conceptions and their derivatives came to prevail, there was less solemnity, less doctrine, less speculation, less theorizing, but all the more practice: here the historical evolution itself is the evolution of ideas relative to public government. Both developments were, in the final resort, conditioned by history—in the one case, because the presuppositions for steady progress were contained in the historical process itself; in the other, because these presuppositions, being historically absent, had to be created by revolutionary force.

Permit me to conclude with a quotation from Sidney Painter which seems particularly appropriate in this context:

> I do not believe that it is too reckless to assert that the basic idea that government should limit the freedom of the individual as little as the general welfare permits, comes from the feudal warrior's insistence on his freedom from restraint. The feudal system fostered individual liberty.

And I may add that it was precisely this feudally inspired individual freedom that provided the fertile ground for those theories which resuscitated the half-forgotten natural man and turned him into a full citizen. To this development I hope to turn in my last lecture.

III

THE HUMANISTIC THESIS

The Emergence of the Citizen

A proper assessment of the forces which initiated the process of releasing the subject from the tutelage into which he was cast by abstract, monolithic doctrine will have to take into account the fact that it was a system that was upheld for centuries and which, above all, was closely linked with the prevalent Christian outlook and cosmology.

It would seem worthwhile to make some general observations. The first is that despite its logical flawlessness and its intellectual consistency, the abstract, descending theme took little, if any, account of the natural, human inclinations of man himself, a standpoint which is indeed not difficult to explain, since the basic elements of the descending theme came from the arsenal of abstract Christian cosmology. The fundamental point is again worth stressing: through baptism man was said to have conquered his own nature and become a new creature; he no longer moved on the plane of ordinary humanity. In other words, the descending theme of government showed all the features of its parent. By its own profession, the descending theme could not and did not make any concessions to the human element which necessarily and assuredly entered into actual government. It was as if government and consequently the subject individual moved within the precincts of concepts and notional abstractions, and not within the realm of human society, with all its earthly concreteness and manifold diversities of the individual's own all-too-human ambitions, volitions, motivations, aspirations, and prejudices. I think it is not too bold to assert that the abstract standpoint, with its governmental adjunct, was an attempt to subject reality to conceptual thinking, to subject—in the public field—the individual's nature to the norm of an a-natural code, to shape and orient natural reality by means of speculative and abstract concepts: in a word, this was literally ideology in its purest form, characterized by the dominance of the idea, by the dominance of the concept to which everything else, including the manifestations of humanity, had to be subordinated.

The doctrinal background of this outlook was the medieval adjustment of the Platonic system. "Platon lui-même n'est nulle part, mais le platonisme est partout," Etienne Gilson once said.[1] You may recall that through Plato the idea of the *nomos,* the idea of realized justice, of the law, had reached its most profound expression. Plato's personification of this idea was the philosopher king who became the embodiment of the *nomos.* This was a sure sign that in this system the individual citizen had receded from a position which would have enabled him to take part in the finding and formulating of the law. The individual became, so to speak, objectivized, no longer fit, because of insufficient qualification—notably lack of knowledge—to try his hand in the making of the laws.[2] In a broad sense, this essentially "antidemocratic" Platonic system became—through its amalgamation with, if not absorption into, the Christian theme—the backcloth of medieval views on political and social organization.[3] The philosopher king as personified law, as the embodiment of the

[1] *La philosophie au Moyen Age des origines patristiques à la fin du* XIVe *siècle* (3d ed.; Paris, 1947), p. 268. See also above p. 22, for Hegel's view.

[2] For this see B. Knauss, *Staat und Mensch in Hellas* (Darmstadt, 1964), p. 106.

[3] In general see Raymond Klibansky, *The Continuity of the Platonic Tradition during the Middle Ages* (London, 1939); see also Tullio Gregory, *Platonismo medievale* (Rome, 1958) and Ivánka, *Plato Christianus,* pp. 301ff. See also the quotation from Heinrich Mitteis, p. 118.

nomos, came to have a status approximating that of divinity and came to constitute the point at which the junction between Platonic and Christian ideas could be, and in actual fact was, established. Argumentation was switched, consequently, to the realm of abstract-speculative thought, which received its especial sanction from the divine halo in which it was enveloped: the element of faith supplied the correlation.[4] That this doctrinal system was, from the point of view of the individual, rigid and inflexible seems self-evident, although it gave to those in "superior authority" considerable latitude.

Looking at the same problem from a different angle, one can also state without fear of contradiction that the governmental system engendered by the abstract-speculative thesis could hardly become the bearer of anything even faintly resembling a constitutional development. Indeed, if the test of any theory of government is its capacity for constitutional development, the theocratic-descending theme of government will be found wanting. Given such a system, I find it difficult to see how a development could take place: if the Ruler is a superior and the individual an inferior who is merely a recipient of the law given to him, it is hard to understand how an evolution of the individual from a mere subject to a citizen could come about. In addition, the system had, as it were, a built-in resistance to change, partly because of its conceptual rigidity and notional inflexibility and partly because of a dogmatic background in which the halo of divinity was always kept in the foreground. Once the view that the Ruler formed an estate of his own became crystallized—or which is the same, once the individual's position was fixed as a *sub/ditus*—this was the end of the matter. Revolution is the only remedy against a determined theocratic-descending form of government.

On the other hand, there are persuasive indications that

---

[4] See above, p. 31.

this system became undermined, became corroded, not from within, but from without. I have dealt at some length in my last lecture with the feudal conceptions which had grown up and operated in close proximity to, yet clearly apart from, the prevalent system that determined the relations between the government and the individual. The feudal system seemed, without much intellectual effort, to give the answer to the problem of how to evolve a kind of government in which at least one stratum of society was provided with the means of participating in matters which concerned all. In a quiet, simple, unobtrusive, but enduring manner the fundamental element of consent here became operative; and on this soil the old-Roman dictum—coined for an entirely different situation—"What touches all must be approved by all" became applicable.

Feudalism was indubitably the most important bridge between the rarefied doctrine of the individual as an inferior and the gradually emerging new thesis of the individual as a full member of the State, as a citizen. But it was not the only one. It is to my mind one of the most interesting phenomena of the period from the late twelfth century on that we find in entirely different and quite unrelated fields, if not a conscious aversion to the objectivized norm, at any rate a greater inclination to pay attention to the individual's own features. With every justification the thirteenth century has been called the century of naturalism, the century in which the natural elements began to assume importance for their own sake. I stress this point because if one is to understand the emergence of a new doctrine, one must see it against the background which reality itself had furnished.

To begin with, the visual arts of the thirteenth century are one such creative epiphenomenon which fertilized the soil and made it receptive to subsequent doctrinal development. As the thirteenth century proceeded, the change from Gothic art to naturalistic realism is noteworthy. One of the best authorities in the history of art has indeed described the Gothic art of the thirteenth century as filled with the spirit of humanism and renaissance.[5] One need look only at some of the products to see at once the striking difference from the preceding portraiture and sculpture. The hitherto stereotyped and typified form gave way to an individualistic and natural portrayal. If you look at, say, Giotto's or Giovanni Pisano's products, you perceive a concrete image and a human personality in all its individuality. The mere abstract image, which depicted no one individual personality, became a realistic image of human proportions with an infinite variety of personal, individual traits. The subject matter of the artist was no longer the idealized norm of the *fidelis christianus,* but the individual as he really and naturally was, or was perceived by the artist. Sculpture and portraiture begin to represent the individual qualities of the human person. Nature was a topic which did not arouse a great deal of excitement and interest before the late twelfth century, a fact which is evidenced in the absence of landscape paintings, yet in the following century it had made its debut and was to remain a perfectly proper genre of artistic creation.[6] What appears to be particularly noteworthy, however, is that among the artists the lay element came more and more to the fore. Of course, for actual building operations the workmen had always been laymen, but from the twelfth century on there is growing evidence that the architectural as well as sculptural work and painting were entrusted

[5] Richard Hamann, *Geschichte der Kunst* (Berlin, 1933), p. 310.

[6] In the twelfth century the literary topos of the *locus amoenus* (the pleasurable place) was, however, frequently the subject of poetic transfiguration and also of the philosophical epic, in which the earthly paradise was depicted, for instance, in Alan of Lille. For this see Curtius, *Europäische Literatur,* pp. 201ff., esp. pp. 204–5. But this *locus amoenus* was an idealized landscape, idealized nature within a carefully confined field. Although no direct lines of communication seem to lead to a correctly understood naturalism of the following century, the fact of this idealization by poets and philosophers is, nevertheless, worth pointing out.

to laymen. It is a feature which we should do well to bear in mind.

It was, furthermore, during the thirteenth century that vernacular literature rapidly increased: and one cannot help thinking that the Latin language was considered inadequate to express all the tender shades of which human feelings were capable. One should bear in mind that Latin and—to use a modern term—the *Geisteswissenschaften* were so intimately linked that the latter entirely depended upon the former. Latin engendered its own linguistic and semantic ethos, far removed from ordinary humanity. It was the vehicle of expression for a specific kind of intellectual pursuit and remained the prerogative of a restricted circle. Latin was perfectly fit for the academic lecture hall, adequate also for the conceptual abstractions, appropriate also for the speculative themes, but the very acceleration of vernacular productions by the turn of the twelfth and thirteenth centuries is, in fact, a measure of the advance made by the popular demand for literature which was written in the language comprehensible to ordinary humanity.[7] Natural and human emotions were capable of being sympathetically portrayed and depicted in a manner for which, by virtue of the paucity of its vocabulary, the Latin of the academics proved insufficient. The vernacular, on the other hand, made it possible for the writer to lay bare the springs of human motivations and actions; it also made possible reflective writing on a scale hitherto not attained; and it was the vernacular which opened the gates to a better understanding of the human psyche. The traditional Latin could quite clearly no longer cope—even if ordinary humanity had understood it—with

[7] Here again the courts of the great feudatories, especially in England and France, provided a suitable public. See *ibid.*, pp. 387f. For specifically religious literature written in the vernacular, also partly connected with the vernacular Bible translations, see Herbert Grundmann, *Religiöse Bewegungen im Mittelalter* (rev. ed.; Darmstadt, 1961), pp. 439ff., especially pp. 449ff.

the subtle variations of human feelings, passions, and motives. Throughout western Europe there is abundant evidence that vernacular prose and poetry increased in quantity and deepened in quality, while Latin remained the language of the scholar. The language of common humanity was the vernacular, which from then on began to enrich literature and enter upon its triumphant career. It is not without interest to note that Dante's contemporary, Giovanni del Virgilio, declared: "The scholar despises the poetry of the vernacular."[8]

In one of the earliest vernacular products touching upon our topic, written by an Italian in the earlier part of the thirteenth century, one detects the emergence of the very theme of the citizen in society. The author was a layman and judge at Brescia, Albertano, who in the thirties of the century wrote his *Libro dell'amore e della dilezione di Dio e del prossimo . . . e della forma dell' onesta vita.*[9] What is so remarkable in this tract is that it contrasts the two main ways of life—the ascetic, contemplative with the active life of a citizen. Although the author admits that there is an overwhelming tradition which favors contemplation and the flight from active life, he nevertheless avows that, for purposes of furthering society and social life in general, contemplation would seem irrelevant: man's nobility of mind demands, he declares, a preference for exerting himself in "communal causes" to living in a state of solitary, contemplative happiness. He does not evaluate the two ways of life, but considers that man may legitimately and freely choose the one or the other, either that of a recluse or that of the citizen.[10] While hitherto "learned" opinion was virtually unanimous in demonstrating the contemplative life as the pinnacle of a Christian's way of living, the Italian, as a

[8] Quoted in Curtius, *Europäische Literatur*, p. 221.
[9] For this see Hans Baron, "Cicero and the Roman civic spirit," *Bulletin of the John Rylands Library*, XXII (Manchester, 1938), 72ff., at 82–83.
[10] See *ibid.*, p. 83.

citizen, layman, and judge, boldly declared that man might choose. His language and his view convincingly indicate the influence of Italian civic life[11] upon a layman who was prompted to write on this kind of topic in the vernacular.

In a different context I have tried in my last lecture to draw attention to the importance of the vernacular within the framework of the law. It seems appropriate to stress this feature in the present context as well, because the first half of the thirteenth century shows—not only in literature, but also in legal productions—that the learned Latin came to be supplanted by the vernacular. One of the earliest products, if not the earliest, was the *Mirror of the Saxons.* The importance of this law book lies in its attempt to present the current law in the vernacular. What is particularly interesting is that the vernacular edition was really a translation from the original Latin by the author himself, Eike von Repgow, and this translation is still preserved in more than 200 complete manuscripts, a measure of its success and also a symptom of the contemporary need to have a law book available in the vernacular.[12] English and French law books written in the vernacular soon followed, all testifying to the necessity to have readily accessible, in a language which clerics as well as laymen could understand, the most crucial element in society, the law. This rendering of the law in the vernacular appears to me to point incontrovertibly to the receptivity of the soil for easily comprehensible books setting forth the hallmark of any civilized society, the law.

That all this constitutes a great change when compared with the clerical predominance in the literature of the high Middle Ages seems clear. No longer did theology and its servant, philosophy, constitute the only worthwhile intellectual pursuit, and no longer was the educated man identical with a cleric: I think one might call this development in

[11] See also below, p. 120.

[12] See Hans Thieme in his Introduction to *Sachsenspiegel,* ed. Claudius von Schwerin (Stuttgart, 1956), pp. 3–4.

creative writing a process of secularization which broadened the subjects as well as the objects of this literature. Literature, in a word, stepped out from the cloistered cell into the broad daylight of common humanity, receiving thereby ever fresh stimulus and impetus. As varied and diversified as humanity is, as varied and diversified were the subjects which the vernacular literature was capable of treating. In more than one respect one can here speak of a release of human forces and faculties which had hitherto lain dormant, hardly, if at all, having had opportunity of forming the very backbone and topos of poetic and prosaic literature.[13] While in the high Middle Ages it was *Memento mori* which set the tone in literature, from the late twelfth century on it was *Memento vivere*. The earlier tone of resignation and flight from the world into eternity was replaced by a *joie de vivre*, by optimism and the appeal to man's own capacities to bring his life on earth to full fruition.[14] Indeed, it has rightly been remarked that the development, at least in vernacular poetry, concerned nothing less than the transition from divinity to humanity: from that time onward it was the human being himself, humanity as it was, which furnished the object of poetic insight and intuition.[15] What this vernacular poetry—and to some extent prose, too—makes abundantly clear is that the writers were perfectly aware of the very sharp distinction between the Christian and the purely secular values, sometimes with a decided affirmation of the latter.[16]

[13] Introducing his chapter "Kulturwandel," K. Hampe, *Das Hochmittelalter* (rev. ed., Gerd Tellenbach; Berlin, 1949), p. 215, said: "Neue Schichten von Laien, die gewiss nicht erst seit gestern weltgewandt und diesseitsfreudig waren, aber nun erst als Kulturträger zu Wort kamen, drängten empor and ergriffen die Zügel."

[14] For this see Friedrich Ranke, *Gott, Welt und Humanität in der deutschen Dichtung des Mittelalters* (Basel, 1953), pp. 13ff., 43ff.

[15] *Ibid.*, p. 45.

[16] For an excellent example see the middle High German verses (printed in *ibid*., p. 52) of the Bavarian knight Engelhart of Adelnburg, in the second decade of the thirteenth century, in which the ennobling of the human body, even at the expense of its soul, is the main point.

In historiography we find a development not unlike that in literature. That the writing of history in the thirteenth century showed some quite remarkable differences in comparison with historiographical works of the earlier medieval period has, in fact, long been recognized, but although this reorientation in historiography reached a preliminary high-water mark in the thirteenth century, its beginnings can be traced to the twelfth.

It will perhaps be useful to recall my observations on the characteristic historiography of the early and high Middle Ages.[17] The change that begins to become so noticeable in the historical works of Otto of Freising did not so much concern the view of the divine government of the world—it would have been too much to expect this: after all, it was no lesser man than Leopold Ranke in the nineteenth century who endorsed this thesis—as the view of the role which man himself played in the historical process, precisely the point which earlier historiography had not reached. In fact, in Otto of Freising one meets not only a terminology that is unfamiliar, but also, and perhaps for the first time, a kind of philosophy of history which not only makes him, as has justifiably been claimed, "a modern thinker," but also ranks him next to Leibniz in his appreciation of the individual and his role.[18] There is a fundamental difference in his approach to history when compared with the traditional, pessimistic, and gloomy view which the chronicler or annalist had of his subject. "We have not set out to write tragedy," he announces, "but a pleasurable history."[19] This was an optimistic, forward-looking standpoint, at least partly explicable by his

---

[17] See above, p, 45.

[18] For this see the fine essay by Joseph Koch, "Die Grundlagen der Geschichtsphilosophie Ottos von Freising," *Geschichtsdenken und Geschichtsbild*, ed. Lammers, pp. 321ff., at pp. 326, 342.

[19] *Ottonis Gesta Friderici* (ed. in M.G.H., *Scriptores Rerum Germanicarum* [1912]) i. 47. 65: "Nos non tragediam, sed iocundam scribere proposuimus hystoriam."

concentration on the individual as the prime agent in the historical process.

This is borne out by his emphasis on the *persona mundialis,* on man as a person of this world, whom he considered from the natural angle. To him there was a development of man and, therefore, also of history, characterized by constant change, in other words, by growth, because man's life constituted a curve which rose to its highest point and then sank again. This view, he tells us, he had from medical science.[20] Nothing, he said, was ever stable or permanent, and man's life showed a striving toward the heights of which he was capable. Change, growth, decay—these were, on the basis of the medical information available, the main features of the individual and, *consequently,* of the historical process initiated and shaped by him. It was, in a word, man's *humanitas,* his being mere man, which was his hallmark,[21] distinguishing him from *animalitas.* This *humanitas* manifested itself in the individuality of man himself.[22] It was what he called the *personalitas* of man,[23] his individuality, which was the motivating as well as moving agent in history. That he also invoked natural observations[24] in addition to medical science should no longer cause surprise. It was perhaps the first time that the individual, man as such, not necessarily as a Christian, had entered into the horizon of a historian, that is, his *humanitas* as such. It would seem superfluous to offer any comments on this in many respects

---

[20] See *ibid.,* 4. 16. ll. 2ff.; Koch, in *Geschichtsdenken und Geschichtsbild,* p. 325.

[21] *Gesta* i. 5. 18: "*Humanitas, quae est integrum hominis.*"

[22] Otto of Freising also termed this *individua substantia;* see *ibid.,* 55. 79; see also p. 78: "individualitas et dissimilitudo"; "individuum et singulare non sunt ad se convertentia, nam omne individuum singulare, sed non omne singulare individuum." For the basic difference between Otto and Gilbert de la Porrée, see Koch, in *Geschichtsdenken und Geschichtsbild,* pp. 343–44.

[23] *Gesta* i. 55. 78. l. 29; *ibid.,* 77. ll. 19f.

[24] *Ibid.,* p. 78; p. 22. ll. 10–11; p. 77. ll. 16f.; p. 79. ll. 25ff.; p. 80. l. 7; et cetera.

quite radical reorientation in historiographical thought although it took considerable time before it had firmly established itself.

Again, entirely unconnected with a doctrine of the individual or, for that matter, unconnected with the arts or vernacular literature or historiography was the phenomenon which deserves at least a passing remark, namely the emergence of what was called in the thirteenth century and has been called ever since the natural sciences. The very term *"natural* sciences" is quite revealing. Just as the artist began to look at man as a human being in all his naturalness, just as vernacular literature began to depict the natural feelings of human beings, just as historiography began to put the individual into the center of the historical process, in the same way observation of natural phenomena and experience as well as the use of experiment began to make their appearance. Once observation and experiment became the *modus procedendi*, the days of the deductive method were numbered; there is little value to depend on authority, on principles, on dogma, because what matters is the minute observation of individual phenomena in the natural world. In fact, it was asserted at the end of the thirteenth century that *auctoritas* induced merely *credulitas*. On the other hand, what was of value was, to express it with the term employed at the time, *experientia*[25] or *experimentum*. It was at Oxford that the Englishman Roger Bacon passionately advocated the new experimental science, termed by him the *scientia experimentalis*.[26]

The advance made by natural science was really quite remarkable and was of great benefit specifically to medical science. For instance, Roger Bacon's ophthalmic work in-

[25] For details see James A. Weisheipl, *The Development of physical theory in the Middle Ages* (London, 1959); Marshall Clagett, *The science of mechanics in the Middle Ages* (Oxford, 1959).

[26] For this information see Eduard J. Dijksterhuis, *The Mechanization of the World Picture*, trans. C. Dikshoorn (Oxford, 1961), pp. 138ff.

cluded, among other things, the rediscovery of the crossing of the optic nerves, the first mention of convex lenses, and the realization that spectacles might remedy visual defects. Interestingly enough, the first medical reference to spectacles comes from the University of Montpellier, where Bernard Gordon in 1305 advocated specially manufactured glass for the correction of eyesight.[27] Anatomy and surgery made equally great strides forward, a point of particular relevance to my topic because, since surgery is, of course, dependent on anatomical knowledge of the human body, there began in the late thirteenth century the anatomical dissection of man. In 1316 the first practical manual of anatomy appeared, written at Bologna by the anatomist Mundinus. I need not specifically mention the radical departure which the anatomical opening of the corpse constituted nor of fierce ecclesiastical opposition to this venture. Over and above all this, rather pronounced empiricism now begins to characterize the mode of inquiry, a point that deserves special mention because the hitherto prevailing deductive method came to be replaced by the inductive method of inquiry.[28]

[27] According to the sermon of a friar, the rediscovery of the art of making spectacles was made twenty years earlier, in about 1285. For all this see Arnold Sorsby, *Modern Ophthalmology* (London, 1963), pp. 5, 29–31; see also Emanuel Rosen, "The invention of Eye Glasses," *Journal of the History of Medicine and Allied Sciences,* XI (1956), 211 (production of eye glasses at Venice). (I am grateful to Dr. F. C. Lane for drawing my attention to this article). For the part played in optical science in general by Robert Grosseteste, Bacon, and John Pecham, see Dijksterhuis, *Mechanization,* pp. 145ff. Parenthetically it should perhaps be mentioned that later there were close interrelations between humanism and medicine, for instance, in Thomas Linacre, whom Thomas More called "dux atque imperator medicae rei"; see R. Schirmer, *Der englische Frühhumanismus* (2d ed.; Tübingen, 1963), pp. 160f.

[28] That the twelfth century prepared the ground for natural-scientific thinking has been recognized more and more in recent years. See the passages in Gregory, *Platonismo medievale,* pp. 135ff.; Tullio Gregory, *L'idea di natura nella filosofia medievale* (Florence, 1965), pp. 17, 26. It would seem, however, that these themes were still firmly embedded in a philosophical, theocentric system. See also M.–Dominique Chenu, *La théologie au douzième siècle* (Paris, 1957), pp. 19–51; Curtius, *Europäische Literatur,* pp. 118ff.; Dijksterhuis, *Mechanization,* pp. 116–25. The statement by Alan of Lille that nature and theology did not contra-

A glance at the writings of Albert the Great, one of the most versatile Dominicans of the mid-thirteenth century, would seem to show the change that came as a result of the study of Aristotelian works on natural philosophy. Even a cursory perusal of his writings proves that themes and topics were now touched upon and treated which had hitherto not constituted the center of scientific interest. Purely natural phenomena now demanded attention—the condition of man in his waking and sleeping state, man's procreation and nutrition, influence of soil and climate upon man's development, the physiology of sex in man and woman, the act of reproduction, sexual psychology,[29] and similar topics now entered the horizon of the writer. Although tradition as a source of knowledge was far from being discarded, observation and experience provided additional sources of knowledge; in fact, Albert came very near to stating that experience and proofs based upon it guaranteed the certainty of knowledge.[30] For in natural science, sense perception and the result-

---

dict each other but were concerned with different things (*non adversa, sed diversa*) (Curtius, *Europäische Literatur*, p. 128) would seem to fit perfectly into the new orientation. The earlier aversion to natural science was partly due to its reputedly close association with magic and sorcery and partly due to "the awe for the authority of tradition" which "dominated the sphere of natural knowledge just as strongly as that of religion"; Dijksterhuis, *Mechanization*, p. 116. It was precisely in this respect that the late twelfth century showed a change: Alan of Lille referred to the wax nose of authority which could be twisted into all shapes and advocated that "one should rely on one's own rational understanding"; *ibid.*, p. 117.

[29] See Arthur Schneider, *Die Psychologie Alberts des Grossen* (in *Beiträge zur Geschichte der Philosophie und Theologie des Mittelalters*, IV, Parts 5–6 [Münster, 1903–6]); Leopold Brandl, *Die Sexualethik des heiligen Albertus Magnus* (Regensburg, 1955), esp. pp. 106ff.

[30] See Albert the Great *De Vegetabilibus* (ed. Carl Jessen [Berlin, 1867]) vi. 1. 1. 339–40: "non de facili aliqua dicere nisi probata per experimentum. Experimentum enim solum certificat in talibus, eo quod de tam particularibus naturis syllogismus haberi non potest." The opening of this sixth book clearly shows Albert's grasp of natural science: "In hoc sexto libro vegetabilium nostrorum magis satisfacimus curiositati studentium quam philosophiae. De particularibus enim philosophia esse non poterit."

ing experience were the only safe guides, and if a conclusion could not be verified by observation and sense perception, Albert counseled that it should be disregarded as an operational principle. Reasoning without experimentation was to him on a lower level than concretely observed evidence, because this appeared to him the most secure way of reaching conclusions in natural science. There is also the remarkable statement of Albert—remarkable only because of the radical departure from theological thinking—that the task of natural science was not simply to describe and accept things, but to inquire into the causes.[31] In other words, the phenomena of nature become accessible to understanding only when the laws of cause and effect are laid bare. That Albert's study of Aristotelian ethics also influenced his own views should at least be mentioned.[32]

I have singled out some quite unrelated fields in which the individual, man himself in his natural make-up, attracted attention. It was the *physis* of man, the nature of the individual himself, which prompted and received close analysis. It was perfectly legitimate that the *fidelis christianus* had been, by definition and by vocation, the proper métier for the theologian and not for the anatomist or natural scientist. Now, however, the physician and scientist joined the company of the theologian and philosopher, but it was a company in which the principle of division of labor operated. The one looked at the individual as a mere *fidelis*, considered him exclusively from the angle of the faith, and worked with the deductive method of reasoning; the other, the physician or natural scientist, looked at the individual as a product of nature and began to work with the inductive method. The resuscitation of the individual as a man of

[31] Albert the Great *De Mineralibus* (ed. Venice, 1517) ii. 1. 1. 139: "*scientiae naturalis* enim non est simpliciter narrata accipere, sed in rebus naturalibus inquirere causas."

[32] For a recent summary of Albert's natural scientific views, see Dijksterhuis, *Mechanization*, pp. 132–33.

nature entailed that he be as worthy of consideration and attention as had been the *fidelis,* who alone had hitherto claimed and obtained a monopoly of treatment. The significance of this division of labor was that the monopolistic attention on the *fidelis* was broken, and he had to share attention with him whose place he was said to have taken.

That part of the individual which for virtually a millenium had been overshadowed—the natural man—was now recovered. What the new development signified can well be classed as the rebirth of the individual as a natural man, as a man of nature, over whom the *fidelis* had for so long cast his shadow. Hitherto, the man of nature, the individual in his natural state, was alleged to have been done away with, to have been wiped out by his baptism.[33] But now this eliminated man of nature was revived, was resuscitated and resurrected, was awakened from the slumber of centuries. He began to stand next to the *fidelis* and began to claim at least the same position and function as his counterpart had had for centuries. It was the mere *homo,* the mere humanity of the individual, upon whom attention came now to be focused. It was the period of *human*ism which was ushered in by the various agencies which I have mentioned.

It will, I hope, be understandable why I have at least alluded

---

[33] It is this standpoint which explains what might be called medieval philosophical (or theological) anthropology, according to which it was the soul only which made man a human person. The main representatives of this view were Hugh of St. Victor, Peter Lombard, Robert Pullus, Peter of Poitiers, Odo of Cambrai, Robert Mélun, et cetera. Hugh, for instance, declared that the soul "ex se et per se habet esse personam" (*Patr. Lat.,* clxxvi. 409[b-c]). The opposite viewpoint in the thirteenth century maintained that both body and soul constituted the human person, for instance, William of Auvergne, who held that the term *Homo* could not be otherwise explained: "nominatur enim homo ab humo, hoc est a corpore terreno. Propter hoc *humanitas* non est anima sola, sed anima est perfectio ipsius corporis"; cited by R. Heinzmann in *Münchener Theologische Zeitschrift,* XVI (1965), 33. It is significant, therefore, that William of Auvergne was the first who developed a rational cosmology entirely independent of theology; see Ueberweg–Geyer, *Grundriss der Geschichte der Philosophie* (12th ed.; Basel, 1951), p. 366.

to these various agencies, in themselves quite unrelated. For there is always an inclination to view a theoretical development in a vacuum instead of seeing it against the actuality of the historical background. What feudalism had already achieved in the public field was, in the thirteenth century, also observable in art, literature, natural science, and so on. Every one of these manifestations of the human mind was totally unrelated to, and unconnected with, each other. It is against this background that one must view the receptivity and the fecundity of the soil for the new Aristotelian theories: they appeared so useful, so eminently sensible, precisely because they expressed theoretically what had already been done in numerous practical ways. To the alert thirteenth-century contemporary, Aristotle seemed to be the perfect *pièce justificative* for what could be perceived in so many contemporary creations, activities, and manifestations of the human mind. I strongly feel that it would be a well-nigh impossible task to explain the rapidity of the Aristotelian advance had it not been for the preparatory and quite diversified agencies. What was done, what was observed, what was discerned, was confirmed, justified, and proved correct by Aristotle's natural philosophy no less than by his political and ethical views.

In this connection I think it advisable to mention at least one of the most notable effects of the Aristotelian influence. Strongly empirical as his natural philosophy was, it infused this empirical-psychological approach into the science of government.[34] While this science had been dominated by a

[34] That physiological considerations infiltrated even into the treatment of theological questions should at least be mentioned. For instance, the Spanish Dominican Ferrarius Catalaunus in 1276 devoted a whole *quaestio* to the problem of whether original sin could be transmitted by the human semen: "Utrum culpa originalis per traducationem seminis traducatur?" Palémon Glorieux, *La littérature quodlibétique de 1260 à 1320*, in *Bibliothèque Thomiste*, V (1925), 108. Another question concerned itself with: "Utrum semen mediante quo contrahitur, sit de substantia generantis et non de superfluo alimento?" (*ibid.*) (I am grateful to my pupil, Mr. P. A. Linehan, of St. John's College, Cambridge, for having drawn my attention to this).

linear exactness of mathematical and syllogistic deductions, the Aristotelian-inspired literature showed a remarkable aversion to this method and an equally remarkable inclination toward the practical, empirical, and observational method. "Even Aristotle had to remind certain pests of his time that an 'educated man' will not expect exactness of the mathematical type in a treatise on politics."[35] What Heinrich Mitteis once called "Political Platonism"[36] was replaced by an Aristotelianism which focused attention on the active, variegated, and multifarious life of ordinary human beings: the replacement of the deductive by the inductive method of reasoning[37] in disciplines other than the natural sciences accounted for the emergence of the new science, that of political science as a social science which dealt with man as he was and as he acted within society. Within this empirical science there was little margin left for the abstract, precise, geometrical formulas so characteristic of the hitherto prevalent mode of thinking. Further, this observational, empirical science did not invoke any standards of absoluteness: the keynote was to be that of relativity.

It is not necessary to describe here in detail the essential ingredients of Aristotle—his concept of Nature with its resultant natural law (so vastly different from the Augustinian concept) and his concept of the citizen, that is, of the individual as a constituent member of the State. Aristotle's thesis that man was a political animal succinctly expressed what was, in any case, somewhat amorphously and dimly felt. Above all, Aristotle's concept of the political animal struck familiar chords, since every literate and educated man was acquainted in any case with the biblical *homo animalis*. And

[35] Eric Voegelin, *The new science of politics* (Chicago, 1952), p. 5.
[36] In *Historische Zeitschrift* (1941), p. 281, he explained it as a doctrine, "der sich das hohe Mittelalter auch ohne spezielle Kenntnis der antiken Texte aus innerer Seelenverwandtschaft nahe fühlen durfte."
[37] This is what Dante called the *ratio inductiva* in his *Monarchia* i. 5.

familiarity with the terminology of a new theory is a presupposition for its success. By distinguishing between the individual as man and the individual as citizen, Aristotle bequeathed to the later medieval world and subsequent generations, one of the most fruitful distinctions: the distinction concerned nothing less than the difference between ethics and politics—the individual as man answering the description postulated by ethics and the individual as citizen answering the description postulated by politics. The Platonic indivisibility of the individual made room for the Aristotelian separability of the individual's functions. The traditional Platonism was replaced by Aristotelianism characterized by the clean separation of ethics and politics. Hitherto, by virtue of the Platonic wholeness point of view, it was conceptually very difficult, if indeed not impossible, to draw a satisfactory distinction between ethics and politics. Plato's *Republic* could equally well be entitled "The Ten Books about Ethics" or "The Ten Books about Politics": politics and ethics were interchangeable with him.[38]

We are so familiar with the concept of politics that we do not realize how recently the word has become part of our language. It is perhaps the surest sign of the state of thinking in the Middle Ages that this term did not exist in the vocabulary of governments and writers on the science of government before the translation of Aristotle by William of Moerbeke in the mid-thirteenth century. And William of Moerbeke had no ready-made term available with which to render the Greek *politeuein* into Latin. He chose or rather coined the new notion of *politizare*, which was the hallmark of the individual in his capacity as a citizen, his capacity to take part in the public affairs of his State, that is to say, of that

[38] See Heinrich Maier in *Wissenschaftliche Politik: eine Einführung in Grundfragen ihrer Tradition und Theorie,* ed. Dieter Oberndörfer (Freiburg, 1962), p. 67, n. 21: "Platon hat menschliche Seele und Gemeinschaftsleben untrennbar verwoben, die zehn Bücher der Politeia könnten sowohl 'Ethik' als auch 'Politik' heissen. Bei Aristoteles kann man die Titel nicht mehr vertauschen."

entity which was conceived as the aggregate of the citizens. The newly coined term *politizare* was not so startlingly novel as one might be inclined to think. Admittedly, as far as I know, the verb was quite novel, but since in the early fifth century Macrobius had popularized the concept of the *virtus politica,* which itself originated with Plotinus, purely philosophic and theological thought in the Middle Ages was not unfamiliar with the concept of the *politicum,* but—and this is the essential point—it had not entered into the vocabulary of governments and writers.[39] One might well observe again that some familiarity with a linguistic term assisted greatly in its becoming general property, although the substance of the term was indeed quite a startling doctrinal novelty.

Similar observations apply to the concept of the citizen, that is, the individual as a participant in matters of government. The term *citizen* had been perfectly familiar: every *civitas* had its *cives;* in the Roman law and in the commentaries by the Roman jurists, the term was equally noted; and quite especially in the northern Italian cities the members were never designated in any other way but by the term *cives,* for their government was civic in every sense. In other words, familiarity with the Roman law and with the actuality of civic government provided a very fertile soil for the theory of citizenship. This is all the more true since, to all intents and purposes, by the thirteenth century the *popolo* of the Italian cities had become a sovereign body, and its members were, in fact, acknowledged as full bearers of rights and duties.[40] It would be quite erroneous, however, to think that

[39] It is interesting to note that a contemporary of Albert and William of Moerbeke, and also a Dominican, the Archbishop of Canterbury, Richard Kilwardby, spoke of politics as *ethica publica,* while the *ethica solitaria* was individual ethics; see Ludwig Baur in *Beiträge zur Geschichte der Philosophie and Theologie des Mittelalters,* IV, Parts 2–3 (1903), 377.

[40] This does not, of course, mean that there was a full-fledged democracy in the modern sense. About this and the composition of the *popolo,* see Ph. Jones, "The city-state in late medieval Italy," *Transactions of the Royal Historical Society* (5th ser., Vol. XV; 1965), pp. 71ff., esp. pp. 74–79, with further literature.

this situation was confined to Italy—far from it. A glance at the charters of any northern medieval king demonstrates that when he addressed them to cities, he addressed them to the citizens of London, York, Rheims, et cetera. What I would like to stress once again is that a quite innocuous designation potently furthered the process by which this designation could become the focal point of a new system: the gulf between the earlier and largely neutral meaning and the later meaningful import of the citizen was bridged by linguistic familiarity with the term *citizen*. In other words, we are presented here with exactly the same feature which I have tried to point out in regard to the preparatory agencies such as feudalism, natural science, the arts, et cetera: here within the precincts of language we also find that quite a number of terms had been familiar, and this familiarity seems to me a vital element if one wishes to understand the accelerated growth of the ascending theme of government and, herewith, the emergence of the individual as a citizen.

This preparatory familiarity with a term or notion is particularly important to bear in mind in connection with the concept of *humanitas*. This, as we shall presently see, became in several respects a vital and fundamental concept for the newly emerging thesis, concentrating as it did upon the essential being of man, upon his natural self as a *human* being, upon his human nature. That this notion gained fairly rapid acceptance was no doubt due to its having been part of the learned vocabulary. In the first place, since early Christian times the christological disputes were exclusively concerned with the nature of Christ as Man and as God, with His human and divine natures. It was precisely in this context that His divinity (*divinitas*) was contrasted with His humanity, with His being mere man.[41] It is not without interest that the one or the other theologian identified Christ's

---

[41] In connection with Christ's *humanitas*, attention should be drawn to Daniel's vision (Dan. 7:13) of the "filius *hominis*," and Christ's own frequent designation of Himself as "Son of Man."

humanity with the flesh, with *caro,* or with the body, the *corpus.*[42] There was no theologian who was not familiar with this concept. To the jurists, too, the notion of *humanitas* was transmitted in the Justinianean codification, in which the term was used frequently—incidentally, the Code in a very prominent place dealt with Christ's *humanitas* as well as His *divinitas*[43]—in the very sense of man's essential being.[44] That Tully, that is Cicero, had employed the concept often should at least be mentioned. Quite apart from these examples, there was, in any case, the customary distinction between *humanitus* and *divinitus,* the one designating "the human manner"; the other, "the divine manner." This is an adverbial usage with which any writer in the Middle Ages was acquainted. The point I wish to make in addition to stressing the crucial term *humanitas,*[45] is that the operative concepts of the newly emerging doctrine concerning the individual had all belonged to the staple vocabulary of the Middle Ages.

It was mainly Thomas Aquinas who, through his flexible adjustments of Aristotelian concepts to the christocentric framework, provided the conceptual and easily comprehensible synthesis by stipulating a "double ordering of things," which had reference to the natural as well as the supranatural order. The idea of a double ordering constituted a major advance in doctrine because, in contrast to the hitherto prevailing thesis, full value could now be ascribed

[42] See, for example, Friedrich Loofs, *Leitfaden zum Studium der Dogmengeschichte* (6th ed., Kurt Aland; Tübingen, 1959), pp. 223ff.
[43] *Codex* i. 1. 8: "in divinitate perfectus . . . et in humanitate perfectus." See also *ibid.,* 17. 2. proem.: "providentia divinae humanitatis."
[44] See, for instance, Dig. 11. 7. 14 (7); Dig. 48. 18. 1 (27); *Codex* i. 14. 9 (7); *ibid.,* v. 16. 27 (1) ("nihil tam peculiare est imperiali majestati quam humanitas"); et cetera. For a mainly philological analysis, see Richard Honig, *Humanitas und Rhetorik in spätrömischen Kaisergesetzen* (Göttingen, 1960); here also the many meanings attached to *humanitas* will be found. See now also K. Büchner, *Vom Bildungswert des Lateinischen* (Wiesbaden, 1965), especially pp. 47–65.
[45] We may also recall the great emphasis which Otto of Freising, for instance, placed in his historical works upon the concept of *humanitas;* see above, p. 111.

to the natural and the supranatural.[46] It would seem impossible to exaggerate the doctrinal achievement of Thomas, who could give full credit to the natural and could juxtapose it with the supranatural. The *fidelis christianus* corresponded to the supranatural; the citizen, to the natural. There was now a veritable dualism of things: the *fidelis* had to share the attention with the *civis,* with the individual who was a full participant in and a natural member of the natural product of the State, of the "congregation of men." It was—in doctrine anyway—Aristotle's and Thomas' definition of a citizen as one partaking in government which supplied the solvent that was to release the inferior subject, the *sub/ditus,* from the superior's tutelage. He who had been overshadowed for so long by the Christian now was resuscitated and reinstated in his full stature: natural man, who had been washed away by baptism, was reborn and as such came to enter, also in theory, the precincts of a correctly understood political doctrine; natural man came to be viewed, at long last, as a constituent member of the natural product, the State. The rebirth of natural man, of the mere *homo* who had been hibernating under the surface for so many centuries, entailed the rebirth of the citizen in the public sphere. To the *renovatio hominis* or *regeneratio hominis* corresponded the *regeneratio civis.* Over and above all that, there is the operational instrument which made possible the rebirth

[46] For some details, especially the underlying conception of natural law, see Ullmann, *Principles of Government,* pp. 243ff. Although I fully agree with Carl Friedrich, *The Philosophy of Law in Historical Perspective* (Chicago, 1958), p. 43 ("I regret the long-established habit of speaking of medieval government as a State when nothing justifies this sort of anachronism. For medieval thought there were princes, lords, rule and government"; see also Carl Friedrich, *Man and His Government* [New York, 1963], p. 549), I myself have always held this view (see Ullmann, *Principles of Government,* p. 87; Ullmann, *History of Political Thought,* p. 137: "The concept of the State was as far removed from the high Middle Ages as the steam engine and electricity"; see also *ibid.,* pp. 17, 140, et cetera), I nevertheless think that Thomas Aquinas' conceptions justify my speaking of the State. They were, after all, not surprising in view of his dependence on Aristotle.

of the individual both as a full man and as a full citizen, that
is, the by then highly fashionable concept of nature.[47] The
wheel, so to speak, had come full circle—first the conquest
of nature by divine grace, as it displayed its effects in baptism,
led to the concept of the *fidelis christianus;* then through the
revival of natural philosophy, notably of Aristotelian themes,
man came to be repossessed and reinstated in his full powers,
as a *homo* in the ethical sphere or as a *civis* in the political
field.

According to Hellenistic thought there were four basic or
cardinal virtues—justice, temperance, prudence, and forti-
tude—which were considered universal, human property and
which determined the character of an action as "virtuous"
if based upon one of them. But doctrine in the Middle Ages
superimposed upon these four virtues the so-called three
theological virtues—faith, hope, and charity—and maintained that an action in order to be "virtuous" must have
been prompted, in addition, by one of these three. The ordinary cardinal virtues which were applicable to any man and
were conditioned by his human nature were, according to
the current medieval doctrine, not true virtues at all and
were designed consequently as "acquired virtues" (*virtutes
acquisitae*), whereas the "true virtues" consisted exclusively
of the three theological ones, because they were "infused"
by divinity (hence, *virtutes infusae*). Thus, within the precincts of the doctrine of virtues, one finds, in fact, a clear
application of the theme that the ordinary human virtues,
not being true virtues, were insufficient for ascribing to an
action virtuous or meritorious character. Nothing reveals the
consistency and integrity of Thomist thought better than the
quite revolutionary thesis that these four ordinary, human,

---

[47] See also Franz Diekamp, *Katholische Dogmatik nach den Grund-
sätzen des heiligen Thomas,* II (Münster, 1950), 44. For the oscillating
concept of nature in Thomas, see also Hans Welzel, *Naturrecht und
materiale Gerechtigkeit* (3d ed.; Göttingen, 1960), pp. 59–60.

cardinal virtues were perfectly sufficient for assigning virtuous character to an action based upon them. They could well be called, Thomas said, "political virtues," because they were the virtues germane to "man as a political animal."[48] Hence, Thomas designated these "political virtues" also as "human virtues,"[49] which were perfectly capable of promoting the general well-being of the community no less than that of the individuals. Transferred to the science of government, Thomas' doctrine entailed that the four ancient, cardinal virtues, having assumed autonomous character, were capable of serving as the basis of the natural product, the State. Precisely because the natural and supranatural—man and Christian—were autonomous, the one could exist without the other.[50]

To Thomas Aquinas, indeed, the notions of man and Christian corresponded to two different categories of thought. Man was a natural product and as such demanded attention:

[48] *Summa Theologiae* (ed. Venice, 1593) i–iiae. qu. 61. art. 5. fol. 127v: "Quia *homo* secundum *suam naturam* est animal politicum, virtutes huiusmodi prout in homine existunt secundum conditionem suae naturae, *politicae vocantur,* prout scilicet homo secundum has virtutes recte se habet in rebus humanis gerendis, secundum quem modum hactenus de his virtutibus locuti sumus." They have reference necessarily only to natural things; see also *ibid.,* qu. 65. art. 2. fol. 134v.

[49] *Ibid.,* qu. 61. art. 1. fol. 125: responsio. For the purely philosophic treatment of the cardinal virtues (it was Macrobius who transmitted the concept) by Alan of Lille in the twelfth century, see *Alain de Lille: Textes inédits,* ed. M. T. d'Alverny (Paris, 1965), p. 303, n. 48. According to Macrobius it was actually the cardinal virtues which made an individual the Ruler over himself; see his *Commentarium in somnium Scipionis* (ed. Leipzig, 1774), I, viii, 51f. ("rector sui").

[50] See Thomas *Summa* qu. 65. art. 2: the human virtues could exist without the theological virtues "sicut fuerunt in multis gentibus." See also the quotation from his commentary on the Sentences in Ullmann, *Principles of Government,* p. 247. In his survey of Thomist doctrine Carl J. Friedrich, *Transcendent Justice* (Durham, N.C., 1964), p. 35, though without reference to Thomas' view on the virtues, rightly points out that his "doctrine embodies a deep and abiding faith in man and his capacity for virtue and self-improvement." For a detailed analysis of the Thomist concept of faith see Reginald Garrigou-Lagrange, *The Theological Virtues,* trans. T. Kempis-Reilly (St. Louis, 1965—).

his naturalness was his hallmark, and as a member of human society he was a social animal. It was Thomas' emphasis on man, on *homo* as such, which gave rise to the characteristically Thomist thesis of *humanitas,* by which he understood the essential being of man himself. The distinction drawn by Aristotle between the individual as man and the individual as a citizen is neatly expressed by Thomas:

> It sometimes happens that someone is a good citizen who has not the quality according to which someone is also a good man, from which follows that the quality according to whether someone is a good man or a good citizen, is not the same.[51]

In other words, ethics and politics do not always coincide; what applies to the one need not apply to the other. To man (*homo*) in the individual sphere the citizen corresponded in the public sphere, and each belonged to the natural order of things.[52]

The specific attention which the individual received in Thomas Aquinas' system explains also the great role which he attributed to the individual conscience: in this, as in so much else, the Angelic Doctor began to set aside the traditional medieval doctrine. In my first lecture I drew attention to the thesis of Gregory the Great, according to which the order of a superior, whether just or unjust, had to be obeyed.[53] Questions of conscience did not apparently enter. Thomas, on the other hand, with his sharp eye for the individual, posed the same question and declared that the order of a superior need not be obeyed if conscience forbade its execution.[54] It is particularly interesting to note his argumentation. The subject, he said, had not to judge the superior

---

[51] Commentary on Aristotle's *Politics* iii. 3.

[52] On this topic see Louis Lachance, *Humanisme politique de saint Thomas d'Aquin* (Paris, 1965), pp. 349ff.

[53] See above, p. 13.

[54] *Quaestiones disputatae de veritate* qu. 17. art. 5: "Conscientia ligabit praecepto praelati in contrario existente," for man's conscience is only bound by a divine precept, but to say that conscience is also bound by superior order is to put the latter on the level of a divine order (*ibid.*).

order itself, but had to justify the execution of the order,[55] because "everyone is bound to examine his own actions in the light of the knowledge which he has from God." The general principle he advocated was that "every man must act in consonance with reason"—"omnis enim homo debet secundum rationem agere"[56]—a principle which persuasively demonstrates the advance in individual ethics and a principle which begins to assert the autonomy of the individual in the moral sphere.

In the history of the relations between man and society, the rebirth of the individual as a full *homo* appears to me one of the major historical achievements of the human mind. It is easy today to sit back and complacently take for granted the constitutionally fixed position of the individual as a citizen, but one forgets too easily that it was not always so and that there was a time spanning the greater part of the Middle Ages, something approaching a millenium, when there was no such thing as a citizen or, for that matter, a political science. We should do well to bear in mind that the very science which now forms a department or a faculty in every university—political science—owes its origin to the same humanistic rebirth of the citizen of the thirteenth century. It was at that time that the very term of *scientia politica* made its appearance, never to disappear again from those branches of knowledge which concern themselves with management of public matters, and political science was called—actually by Thomas Aquinas—the most fundamental and architectonic of all sciences, because without it human philosophy would be, according to Thomas, incomplete: political science was, to him, applied human reason

[55] *Ibid., ad* 4: "Subditus non habet judicare depraecepto praelati, sed de impletione praecepti, quae ad ipsum spectat." In his *Summa* qu. 96. art. 1, he said: "judicium divinum quod est judicium conscientiae."

[56] *Ibid., ad* 4. For the philosophic treatment of conscience by Thomas, see O. Lottin, *Psychologie et Morale au XIIe et XIIIe siècles,* II (Louvain-Gembloux, 1948), 222–35.

which understood and brought about man's political community. The birth of political science was conditioned by the rebirth of man as a political animal, which also entailed its human and empirical character, for within it the experience of man and his natural reasoning mattered. As Thomas tells us, political science formed part of the human sciences and therefore "aimed at imitating nature." It was a veritable reversal of things: from the *conquest* of nature effected through baptism to the *imitation* of nature.

There was still more to the development of political science. A new kind of literature arrived on the scene. This was monographic literature, specially devoted to this topic, which began to deal with those very questions which are to this day the staple food of any course in political science. What I would like to stress is that the publicistic-monographic literature had to begin *ab ovo*, had to investigate the most rudimentary questions, not by a facile recourse to a given set of principles, but by the establishment of its own criteria, its own values, its own terms of reference. It was as if a new continent had been discovered—the mere and so much despised *homo* was elevated in the public sphere to a being in his own right, or if we wish to use traditional terminology, he himself became a "superior." The rebirth of man concerned the rebirth of his natural humanity, with its innumerable ramifications and potentialities: it concerned man as he was created by nature.

One hardly appreciates in the twentieth century what a deep impact this renaissance of man made, nay, what a chasm was opened between this way of thinking and the traditional theocentric manner. Let us recall again the gulf that existed in Pauline and Christian doctrine between the natural man and the Christian; let us also recall the undisputed view that the baptized man had conceptually done away with the man of nature.[57] In a number of places Paul

[57] See above, p. 7.

had drawn the contrast between the *homo animalis* and the *homo spiritualis*,[58] going so far as to say that "the spiritual man judges all things, yet he himself is judged by no man."[59] The core of the new doctrine, however, was precisely this— that natural man himself, having been reborn and reinstated, had emerged as an independent, autonomous unit within the framework of the natural order. None saw more clearly than Boniface VIII the conceptual assault on hitherto unimpeachable and undisputed theses concerning public power in general and the latent deadly threat to ecclesiastical power in particular. His decree *Unam sanctam*[60] customarily receives a prominent place in treatises on political thought and is depicted as an example of the overbearing urge to power on the part of the papacy. I would not dispute that the decree can bear this interpretation, but I would also think that it assumes far greater—and hitherto unnoticed— historical significance when thrown against the ideological background which has just engaged us. The decree, in actual fact, constitutes an apotheosis of the *homo spiritualis* and culminates in the reassertion of the "spiritual man" (and consequently of "spiritual power") as the measure and judge of all things. It would seem to me that this highly charged formulation of the unique function and position of the "spiritual man" and of the attendant consequences in the ecclesiastical field would have recalled vividly and impressively to a contemporary the very sharp contrast that existed between him and the "natural man." This was at least one— and certainly not unimportant—reason for issuing the decree; it was to warn contemporaries, by a solemnly executed and broadcast statement, against the latent dangers which the

[58] See I Cor. 2:14; also 15:44,46—the term *homo animalis* is translated in both the Authorized Version and the Douay Version as *natural man.*

[59] I Cor. 2:14–15.

[60] Text conveniently available in Mirbt, *Quellen,* pp. 210–11; translated also by Brian Tierney, *The Crisis of Church and State 1050–1300* (Englewood Cliffs, N.J., 1964), pp. 188–89.

recent ideological development, with its emphasis on natural man, harbored. The forceful reassertion of the *homo spiritualis* over and above the *homo animalis*—for the former makes sense only in relation to the latter—and the consequent buttressing of "spiritual power" constituted the papal challenge to the new orientation;[61] and this quite especially so when one attends to the contrast which Boniface VIII drew between human and divine power in this very same context. For the essential point was that in the new theory man himself was naturally the legitimate and rightful bearer of power, and this power was of natural, not of divine, origin. However forcefully expressed an opposition may be, it nevertheless can rarely deflect an ideological development from its path.

That the development ran its course and that Boniface— or for that matter anybody else—was unable to stem the advance can be seen from the views expressed by his own contemporaries. One of the masters of the University of Paris, Jean Quidort (Johannes Parisiensis), wrote at the very time when Boniface VIII had published his *Unam sanctam*. The length of his treatise stands somewhat in inverse proportion to its importance: in the modern edition it has fewer than 100 pages,[62] but the tract seems to me to put forward some very influential themes. On the basis of Aristotelianism the author realized the full potentialities of the distinction between the *fideles* and *cives*. This vital distinction assumes

[61] From his point of view the attack was quite understandable, notably when due consideration is given to the new idea of natural law, for this law does not and cannot distinguish between Christians and non-Christians, between orthodox and heterodox, between Frenchmen and Romans, and so forth. It was to be applicable to any human creature, regardless of any further qualification. It would seem that the famous last sentence of *Unam sanctam*—it is necessary for every human creature to be subjected to the Roman pontiff—had precisely this in mind, since what mattered was the "spiritual man"—natural man and natural law could have no standing in this scheme of things.

[62] Jean Leclercq, *Jean de Paris et l'ecclésiologie du XIII siècle* (Paris, 1942), ed. pp. 173–260.

in John's tract the significance of a fundamental operational principle. The *fideles,* he declared, were united by the bond of faith and were not in need of what he significantly called a *politia communis,* that is, a common political structure, but for the citizens this *politia communis* was essential. What he wished to express with this statement was that political power belonged to the citizens and not to the faithful, who, precisely because they had faith, were directed and guided, not by them themselves, but by superior authority. In other words, they were, as faithful Christians, mere subjects, and because they were the faithful, they accepted the law from the superior, in whose function as law-giver they had faith. The position of individuals in their capacity as citizens, however, was quite different, since as citizens they "naturally" had a right to take part in the government of their own *politia communis.*

In John of Paris' tract one witnesses the emergence of the proper concept of citizenship, and what makes the tract so appealing is that at once the empirical argument comes to the fore. An empirical argument cannot be tied to fixed norms, and John's empirical argument had none of the once-and-for-all validity of a norm. There were, he said, *diversae politiae,* that is, diverse political structures, because different languages, different climates, different geographical conditions, and so on had made the diversity of political structures necessary. There was just no one political structure applicable to all societies, and it is significant that John of Paris added that for the society of the faithful there was every justification for one and the same structure. The important point here is that the rigidity of political thought gave way to flexibility; the postulate of a dogmatic principle yielded to the variety and diversity of human development according to natural conditions; the linear, geometrical point of view was replaced by one that focuses attention upon the multifariousness of humanity as it manifested itself in its natural surroundings. Into the place of the hitherto prevalent monolithic thesis of absoluteness stepped the dominant note of relativity.

Precisely because the State was the outcome of what John of Paris called the "natural instinct" (*instinctus naturalis*) of individuals to form themselves into a community, the citizens themselves made up the State. This is indeed language which one has not had much occasion to hear before, for the citizens—and not the faithful—were the bearers of the idea of the State as well as its practical manipulators: as he avowed, they elected the king, who was so much bound to them that his power could also be taken from him by the constituent elements of the State, by the citizens.

In assessing the advance of political reasoning toward what might well be called a Lockean position, one should also appreciate, I think, the radical view of John of Paris concerning the property of the individuals themselves, hitherto held to have been an issue of divine grace and consequently at the disposal of those who ruled "by the grace of God."[63] John's view that individuals (whom he called *personae singulares*)[64] had a right to property which was not with impunity to be interfered with by superior authority— because it was acquired by their own efforts—may indeed be called a pre-Lockean thesis of the rights of individuals to property by the law of nature.[65] It was still more novel for John to say that the citizens had it in their own power to shape the destiny of their own State: the *tota vita*,

[63] See above, p. 38.

[64] Leclercq, *Jean de Paris*, cap. VII, p. 189.

[65] It may be recalled that a House of Commons petition in 1609 declared, among other things, that all free subjects may freely inherit the free exercise of their industry in the callings by which they live. If one compares this with John of Paris' view on the acquisition and disposal of private property, one will notice not only a similarity of reasoning, but also one of the terms employed; see *ibid.*: property acquired by individuals through their skill, work, and industry is removed from anyone's jurisdiction, and "everyone is freely entitled to settle, manage, alienate, retain and dispose of his own property."

the totality of life in the State, was made, he said, the subject matter of the citizens' own legislation. Law was becoming a matter of direct concern to the citizens, and the ingredient which imparted enforceability to the law was the citizens' consent. The citizen was becoming the judge and master of his own social and political life, because he was the bearer of the idea of the State. The idea of the mere subject individual as a recipient of orders, decrees, and laws was receding into the background. It was, in other words, the citizens' own insight into the needs of their own State which guaranteed the well-being (or what he called the *bene vivere*) of the whole of the State. The idea of lawmaking by the citizens takes the place of the former idea of law-giving by superior authority to the subjects. This development would hardly have been possible without the antecedent rebirth of the individual as man and the resulting humanism.

Perhaps the most consistent exponent of the humanistic thesis was Dante. To him the *humana civilitas*, mankind as such, was a basic operational element. I do not think it necessary to draw attention specifically to the profundity of this notion which, precisely because of its economy of words, might well hide its depth and maturity: it is the purely human element which Dante wishes to stress in the concept of *civilitas*.[66] The glowing tribute which on several occasions Dante pays to Aristotle is indeed fully comprehensible— Aristotle, the "maestro e duca delle gente umana. . . . il maestro e l'artifice che ne dimostra il fine della umana vita."[67] It was mankind itself, the human race itself, consisting not merely of Christians, but also of Muslims, Jews, and pagans, with which he was concerned. Man alone was the constituent member of the *humana civilitas*, and from this should

[66] One begins to realize the advance when one compares Dante's *civilitas* with John of Salisbury's *civilitas*, by which he meant no more than civility.

[67] *Convivio* iv. 6.

be distinguished, Dante avows, the *christianitas,* which to him was the supranatural complement of the *humana civilitas.* But while nature itself brought forth the latter, the *christianitas,* as Dante had it, was "not the effect of nature." The consequence was unambiguously stated: to each of these two bodies different norms, different modes of operation, different sets of principles were applicable. What did not apply to the concept of *christianitas* was the law of nature. The application of the Thomist double ordering of things explains Dante's view that man pursued a twofold aim: as a citizen, a this-worldly and natural end; as a Christian, an other-worldly supranatural aim. *Humanitas* and *christianitas* were two quite separate notions. Man's distinguishing mark Dante found to be his intellectual powers, which were to him the standard, rule, and measure of man's actions. Behind these assertions stood Dante's passionate belief in man's free will, the exercise of which flowed from the liberty of man, "which is the greatest gift of God conferred on human nature." A statement such as this demonstrates how far political philosophy had advanced.

This is perhaps the first time that the theme of human liberty was sounded, a liberty which was grounded in human nature and related to the choice of the means by which man as a citizen could achieve his natural end within human society.[68] Liberty was for Dante the guarantee that man would achieve felicity on this earth, because only that was free, he declared, which existed for its own sake, not for the sake of something or somebody else. It was the assertion of man's autonomy: man was perfectly capable of looking after himself.[69] The pursuit of human ends for their own sakes was the message which Dante wished to convey, and that

[68] *Monarchia* i. 12: "The human race when most free, is in the best state of health."

[69] In this context Dante's arguments in *Monarchia* iii. 4 concerning the inner force, the *motor,* should be mentioned.

human activity which pursued these ends Dante called
politizare—acting in a political manner as a full-fledged
citizen, as a member of the *humana civilitas*.[70] It was this
human activity by which the potentialities of humanity and
of man himself were capable of being realized, for "the function of any right government is to see that men exist for
their own sakes." The liberalization of man's germane faculties for the sake of his self-realization within society was, in
the last analysis, the basic theme of Dante,[71] for he held that
"right governments contemplate freedom."[72] To him government was, therefore, a service performed for the people—the
government was the *minister omnium,* the servant of all, a
point of view which indeed was a far cry from the earlier
Pauline concept of the Ruler as the *minister Dei*. The wheel
had come full circle: the government was no longer the
superior that laid down and gave the law to a subjected
mankind, but liberated man himself was to see in the government his servant and the protector of his own interests.
Dante's themes are the apotheosis of the reborn man; they
constitute the climax of the humanistic efforts to liberate
man for his own sake, to free humanity for its own sake, by
the appeal to man's own capacity of self-realization.

The humanistic philosophy of Dante may suitably be
supplemented by the political and legal philosophy of Marsiglio of Padua, in whose work one can see not only the
progress but also the maturity which the new science, the
scientia politica, had reached. The real bearer of political

[70] *Ibid.,* i. 12.
[71] From here one will also understand Dante's theme of a twofold
reformation—one a political reformation concerning society, the other a
religious regeneration concerning the individual—as set forth in his
Purgatorio i. 22ff. and xxxi. 103ff. See also Konrad Burdach, *Vom
Mittelalter zur Reformation,* III, Part II (Berlin, 1926–32), 302f.; Ernst
Kantorowicz, *The King's Two Bodies* (Princeton, 1957), pp. 469f.
[72] *Monarchia* i. 12: "Citizens are not there for the sake of governors,
nor the nation for the sake of the king, but conversely the governors for
the sake of the *citizens,* the king for the sake of the nation."

power was to him the *universitas civium*—I do not think that it is necessary to point out the crucial difference between this term and the *universitas fidelium*—and this corporation of the citizens Marsiglio called most significantly the human legislator, the *legislator humanus,* in which the accent lay on the human element. What in Dante's humanistic philosophy was, on a universal scale, the *humana civilitas* was in Marsiglio's political jurisprudence the *legislator humanus.* This corporation or community of citizens was the State, which was not something that was ordained from high or given by a superior, but was the citizens' own. And the main function of the State was to make laws—hence, Marsiglio's identification of the *universitas civium* with the *legislator humanus,* which means one thing only, namely that the State was its own legislator. Because the laws were made by the citizens as the sole constituent members of the State, they were human laws; no longer were the laws of the State given by a superior standing outside and above the citizens. Again, no novelty can be detected in the concept of *universitas* or that of the *cives*: the novelty consisted in making one concept out of the two, and in its succinct formula this combination gave birth to a whole crop of new ideas.

Non-human laws, that is, divine laws, could by their very nature have no claim to be called proper laws, because they presupposed a subject, and a subject could give no consent. It is the element of consent which seems to me the really pivotal one in Marsiglio's jurisprudential system, for it alone made a law what it was—an enforceable rule of action because it was so willed by the citizens themselves. The distance between the traditional standpoint and Marsiglio's can be measured when due consideration is given to his statement that the law was an *oculus ex multis oculis*— it would be difficult to improve upon this: the many eyes of the citizens perceived the need for an injunction or prohibition which, because seen, i.e., willed by the many, became one eye in the shape of the law. In the traditional doctrine it was the faith of the subjects which was the material ingredient of the law; now this faith was replaced by consent as the expression of the citizens' will, which thereby imparts coercive character to the law. The law was fetched down from the heavens and put into the hands of the citizens, now considered quite capable of managing their own lives on the basis of their own insights into the needs of their own State. Acting in their totality as a community of citizens, they now possessed sovereignty, because they alone were held to be the bearers of original power: no longer was the sovereign (=superior) set above the subjects. Original power resided with the citizens—the hallmark of the ascending theme of government.

In the postulate of the citizens' freedom, Marsiglio advances the standing of the citizens and thereby demonstrates how far he has removed political doctrine from the antecedent theses relative to the standing of the individual. Often he says that "any citizen must be free,"[73] and this freedom concerns the consent of the citizens to the restraints prescribed by the laws made by them themselves. This freedom of the citizens results from Marsiglio's view of the individual's sense of responsibility, self-restraint, and maturity of judgment, which are a presupposition for active participation in government.

At least as important as his political doctrine of responsible freedom to govern is the corollary which Marsiglio states, namely the freedom of the individual to interpret the Bible as seems best to him. The aversion to subscribing uncritically to a point of view merely because it is contained in tradition or in an authoritative pronouncement is nothing but the

[73] See, for instance, *Defensor Pacis,* trans. Alan Gewirth (Chicago, 1956), i. 12. 16. 47 ("*Quilibet civis liber esse debet*"): "That law is better observed *by every citizen* which each one seems to have imposed upon himself . . . ," et cetera.

postulate of the belief in the individual's own intellectual capacity to understand the Bible and draw his own conclusions, quite apart and beyond tradition or authority.[74] Further, both the freedom of the citizen and of the individual lead Marsiglio to introduce the principle of numerical majority into the doctrinal literature on politics, though still in conjunction with the qualitative principle.[75]

Because the State is, for Marsiglio, the citizens' own, a naturally growing body composed of natural human beings, the further important consequence is that there is no *prima facie* means to distinguish among the citizens in their capacity as citizens.[76] It is necessary to mention this in order to bring out the essential difference between the concept of the State and that of the Church. The latter was, to be sure, composed of all the faithful members, without distinction, but for governmental purposes there was the basic differentiation between the ordained and unordained faithful members, between the clergy and the laity. Within the concept of the State and its constituent citizens no such distinction could be drawn—the citizen had no charismatic qualities, but was simply human, and for this reason was autonomous and independent.[77] Thereby, the traditional

[74] See *ibid.*, ii. 28. 6. 376: "It is indeed remarkable if we are obliged to believe the authority of the glossators rather than Christ, whoever be that glossator, even a saint . . ."; *ibid.*, p. 371: "infallible reason grounded in Scripture"; et cetera. Perhaps Gewirth. i. 75, goes a little too far in asserting that Marsiglio is "clearly a precursor of the individualism of the Reformation."

[75] For earlier quantitative majority see above, pp. 34f. and for Marsiglio see also E. Lewis in *Speculum*, XXXVIII (1963), 566, n. 98.

[76] This does not, of course, mean that there is equality in regard to ability.

[77] In some ways this, too, is a reversal of the antecedent doctrine. Formerly (see above, p. 14) it was held that all men were equal, but it was an equality which did not operate within the sphere of government, where *potestas* and *scientia* counted. According to Marsiglio there was a natural inequality of men, but as citizens, as men partaking in government, there was no distinction. It is precisely in regard to *scientia* that Marsiglio states (*Defensor Pacis* i. 13. 4. 52): "it does not follow that the wise can discern what should be enacted better than the whole multitude, in which

medieval barrier between clergy and laity, a barrier which divided medieval Christendom, was torn down. No privileges were attributable to a citizen. There was, in fact, a perfect expression of the citizens' and, therefore, of the State's sovereignty in the Bartolist formula of the *civitas sibi princeps*, of the State's being its own prince. This was only a juristic formulation of what Marsiglio had set forth as the sovereignty of the people, the sovereignty of the citizens themselves.

It would give quite an erroneous impression were one to assume that this thesis of the renaissance of man and, consequently, of the rebirth of the citizen was confined to the one or the other "radical" thinker. Numerous witnesses of a less radical bent can be cited who put forward themes and theses in essential agreement with their more radical contemporaries. For instance, Giles of Rome, in his tract written for the French king Philip IV, moved entirely within the Aristotelean-Thomist conceptions when he spoke of the State (the *civitas*) as "something natural," the stability and prosperity of which resulted "from the industry and works of the men themselves who composed it."[78] In other words, Giles focuses attention upon the human character of the State, upon the man-directed, this-worldly body of citizens. The jurist Durandus de San Porciano exactly contemporaneously with Marsiglio and as neatly and as clearly as one

the wise are included together with the less learned"; or *ibid.*, 5. 53, and 6. 53–54: "If any citizen thinks that something should be added, subtracted, changed or completely rejected, he can say so, since this means the law will be more usefully ordained"; et cetera.

[78] Egidius Romanus *De regimine principum* (ed. Rome, 1556) II pars. iii. 32. 320: "Sciendum est quod civitas sit aliquo modo quid naturale, eo, quod *naturalem* habemus *impetum* ad civitatem constituendam, non tamen efficitur nec perficitur nisi ex opera et industria hominum"; in *ibid.*, iii. 1. 1, it is simply an "opus humanum." See also *ibid.*, fol. 321v.: "Debet rex, si sit verus et rectus, idem intendere in *uno cive* et in *tota civitate* et in regno toto." In *ibid.*, cap. 34, 322v., he very neatly distinguishes, in Aristotelian manner, between "the good man" and "the good citizen."

might wish drew a distinction between the individuals as
Christians and as citizens, thus spelling out the Thomist
thesis in juristic terms. Durandus maintained—and I do not
think that Marsiglio would have disagreed with him—that
the secular power had jurisdiction over men, not in their capacity as Christians, but solely as citizens, because there was
a secular legitimate power also among non-Christians, but
the spiritual power confined its jurisdiction to "faithful Christians."[79] Indeed, the Thomist double ordering was now expressed in terms of the current jurisprudential doctrines: the
individual was now juristically split up into a Christian and
a citizen. The Aristotelian atomization of man, the carving
up of man's various functions and the norms to which he was
subjected, now also received its doctrinal application in the
framework of legal procedure.

If we allow ourselves a glance at the fifteenth century, it
becomes clear that the individual came to be more and more
considered as the instrument of nature itself: man led by
nature—*duce naturae*—was himself responsible for all the
manifestations and emanations of an orderly life within the
State. Social life once more had become man's own creation.
It was in the power of man acting as a citizen to furnish
those essentials which guaranteed the continued existence
of the State. For the citizen was he who took part in public
business—"particeps publici muneris"—and while the idea
of justice, as framed and fixed by the citizens, was "the
foundation of human society" (*fundamentum humanae
societatis*), the end of "the popular State," the State of the
people itself, was liberty.[80] The citizens were in no need of
any agencies outside themselves.[81] And the main feature of

[79] See the long quotation of his passage in Wilks, *The Problem of
Sovereignty,* p. 139, n. 2, ending in: "Quilibet laicus christianus est
utrique judicio subditus, uni ut civis, alii ut christianus."
[80] Franciscus Patricius Senensis *De reipublicae institutione* (ed. Paris,
1575) i. 3. 13ff.; the quotations in the text on pp. 14v, 16, and 16v.
[81] *Ibid.,* p. 15: "Nam si cives optime animati, aequi bonique studio
adducti ad rempublicam accederent, supervacua praecepta essent quibus
humana societas instituitur."

the popular State—the *popularis status*—was equality of its citizens before the law, and this equality was expressed by the novel term *isonomia*.[82] We stand indeed on the threshold of the modern era. Man's own human dignity was now recognized at long last in its full human value and potentiality. While Paolo Vergerio begins the rational inquiry into the psychology of man, Palmieri treats of the *Vita Civile*, and Gianozzo Manetti and Pico della Mirandolla throw light on the excellence and dignity of man[83]—the classic humanist counterpart to the classic medieval product *On the Misery of Human Existence*.[84]

It would be an exciting and fascinating task to pursue the numerous ramifications entailed in the rebirth of man and the consequential re-emergence of the citizen, for on the not-too-distant horizon was the Renaissance, with its professed apotheosis of the individual. But the pursuit of the manifold implications, applications, and filiations which the renaissance of man and of the citizen brought forth must be left to those who are better qualified than I am. One passing reference I hope you will allow me, and that is that the rediscovery of man in his naturalness and real being would seem to me to have conditioned also the renaissance of ancient literature. As a medievalist I am inclined to think that as a historical phenomenon Renaissance humanism

[82] *Ibid.,* p. 16: "Dicitur enim *isonomia* quasi juris equalitas, quando in republica in qua multitudo dominatur, aequo inter omnes jure omnia administranda sunt . . . huius finis est libertas." How this highly interesting concept of *isonomia* came again to be operational, I do not know. For the different interpretations in Greek political thought, see G. Vlastos, "Isonomia Politike," *Isonomia: Studien zur Gleichheitsvorstellung im griechischen Denken,* ed. Jürgen Mau and Ernst G. Schmidt (Berlin, 1964), pp. 1–2, 15ff. In fact, it seems that *isonomia* was considered the basic idea underlying democracy; see Victor Ehrenberg, s.v., in August Pauly, *Real-Encyclopädie der classischen Altertumswissenschaft,* ed. Georg Wissowa, suppl. vol. VII (1940), cols. 293–301.

[83] For a twelfth-century precursor (*dignitas hominis etiam secundum corpus*) see Gregory *L'idea di natura nella filosofia medievale* p. 33.

[84] By Innocent III. The full title is: *De contemptu mundi sive de miseria conditionis humanae, Patr. Lat.* ccxvii. 701ff.; new edition by M. Maccarone (Lucca, 1955).

should not be isolated from its historical context: isolation of its purely cultural and literary aspects leads to a one-sided and, hence, an unhistoric picture full of *schöngeistige* reflexions. It is now generally recognized that much of ancient literature was familiar throughout the Middle Ages, and the flood of classical learning became quite respectable from the twelfth century on. But classical authors were not taken as models, they did not serve as guides, they did not supply new norms, because the real medieval problem was how to fit the emanation of the ancient (pagan) mind into the all-pervading Christian theme. Leaving aside some isolated instances of hostility to classical authors—for instance, the belief that Homer or Vergil was a criminal—medieval learning viewed them, so to speak, *sub specie aeternitatis*, viewed them as intellectual products: if they could be shown to be consonant with the Christian faith, they were to be "canonized," but if they were opposed to the tenets of faith, they should be consigned to oblivion.

Renaissance humanism, on the other hand, had few problems of fitting ancient products into the Christian framework, for this humanism fully realized the potentialities of the ancients as avenues to a better understanding of man himself, of him who had been overshadowed hitherto by the faithful Christian. In other words, the ancient writers could, as indeed they did, become patterns and models; the view may be tentatively expressed that medieval familiarity with the classical authors greatly facilitated their becoming models and that Renaissance humanism was powerfully conditioned by the antecedent humanism of what might well be called a political order, that is, the renaissance of man himself as a full-fledged citizen, with the consequential emphasis on the human society, the State.

Two specific points arise from this reflection. The first is the infiltration of the humanist point of view into historiography. Since man was now recognized in his full stature and perceived as a creation of nature—and after all, the creator of nature was God Himself—it was considered not only permissible but also imperative to bring man's own part in the historical process into clearer relief than was possible in medieval annalistic literature. A historiographic standpoint such as that of Otto of Freising was no longer merely an indication of things to come, but had become the more or less accepted point of view in the late Middle Ages. Historiography now begins to show with remarkable clarity how humanized, if I may use this term, historical writing had become and also how rapidly the allegedly objective point of view gave way to a proper assessment of the prime mover of history, of man himself. This orientation toward an apprehension and comprehension of the part played by the individual himself, the appraisal of the human element in history, is, however, only one epiphenomenon of the resuscitated man.[85]

The other point concerns the increased emphasis which the individual received in the religious sphere. Here again the objective and institutionalized form of the faith was to make room for a subjective and personal approach to divinity. This internalization of the faith—if I may so call this process—seems to me responsible for the reinvigoration of the religious life in the fifteenth century and beyond: its manifestations were in some respects clearly linked with the medieval past, yet showed features which were explicable only by the heightened attention which the individual Christian had received. The *Devotio moderna,* with its stress on the imitation of Christ, aimed precisely at enriching the internal religious life of the individual. Not the least significant

[85] But assuredly one epiphenomenon only, for although not directly bearing upon my topic, mention should at least be made of such features as the beginnings of personal diaries in the fourteenth century, personal memoirs, the cultivation of the epistolary style, and the like. What also is quite significant is that architects and builders were publicly recognized as creative organs: Charles IV had the busts of his architects and builders erected in the Cathedral of Prague.

vehicle which contributed to this internalization of the faith
was the vernacular language, both in sermons and popular
literature. That the latter reached a very high standard in
the fifteenth century is both acknowledged and explicable.
Perhaps the most convincing proof of the hungry receptivity
of the laity for religious nourishment lay in the numerous
translations of the Bible into the vernacular throughout the
length and breadth of western Europe. The need for a
vernacular Bible was one aspect of the late medieval desire to
return to the original.

These considerations may further offer an explanation for
the aversion to the theological speculations of medieval
scholasticism, one of the chief features of many humanists.
These speculations, conducted as they were, so to speak, on
a geometrical plane, appeared to the humanists a purely
mechanical, if not mechanistic, way of dealing with central
questions of the individual's religious life. The force of
Augustine's passage

> Men go to admire the heights of the mountains, the great
> floods of the ocean, the courses of rivers, the shores of the sea
> and the orbits of the stars, and neglect themselves[86]

or the same saint's exclamation

> Truth dwells inside Man[87]

was not lost on the humanists. The return to classical pagan
authors was accompanied by a return to classical Christian
writers, of whom none received greater attention than Augustine.[88] Here as there the humanist watchword was: back to
the original and away from the artificial incrustations of

[86] Quoted in Paul O. Kristeller, *Renaissance Thought* (New York,
1961), p. 125. For stimulating observations see pp. 70ff.

[87] Augustine *De vera religione* xxxix. 72 (Migne, *Patr. Lat.*, xxxiv.
154). The whole passage runs: "Noli foras ire, in teipsum redi: in
interiore homine habitat veritas."

[88] Burdach, *Vom Mittelalter*, III, Part II, p. 101, has finely expressed
this increased influence of Augustine: "Diese Quelle [that is, Augustine]
ist jetzt endlich vom Schutt befreit und spendet ihr Wasser ungetrübt."

medieval lore. In brief, the direct link between the individual and divinity, without the mediatory role of ecclesiastical officers, became the pivotal point of man's religious life.

From the standpoint of the historical-constitutional development, however, it must be said that the implementation of the new thesis against the encrusted, old, and traditional themes encountered severe resistance, frequently leading to bloody conflicts. That the release of the individual from the tutelage into which the medieval *Munt* had forced him took so long a time, reaching right down to the nineteenth century if not beyond, is indeed not difficult to understand. This retarded process was a measure of the strength which the twin pillars of the Establishment, throne and altar, were always able to muster. The resistance of the traditional-conservative forces to the attempted translation of the ascending theme of government into practice led to revolution. I would think that the device which the French Revolution and, probably in its wake, the Russian Revolution in our own day, adopted was not a mere frill or embellishment, but one with deep ideological significance—the device, that is, of prefixing the term "Citizen" to the surname, so that there were Citizen Mirabeau, Citizen Danton, and the like, and Citizen Plekhanov, Citizen Romanow, and so on. I venture to think that in this metamorphosis of the subject and in his re-emergence as a citizen a long historical development is mirrored in an exemplary manner. It needed a revolution to effect the change, a change which reflected as clearly as one might wish the radically different conceptions, in themselves historically conditioned, of the standing of the individual in society.

We have now reached the end of a long and perhaps somewhat wearisome journey which has attempted to highlight and bring into sharper focus a problem of perennial

interest. That the standing of the individual within society
and the character of society itself have since the eighteenth
century been not only theoretical problems but also, and
perhaps even more so, severely practical ones should not
prevent our inquiring into the historical situation which in
actual fact made the relation of the individual to his society
a problem of political magnitude. Permit me, therefore, to
offer some brief conclusions.

First, although it might seem that the descending thesis
of government and law, prevalent and virtually undisputed
as it was in the high Middle Ages, had little to contribute,
it nevertheless transmitted to later generations one very
precious legacy, and that is the idea of the supremacy of
law, the idea of the rule of law. Ideas originate, develop,
and exercise influence only within historically conditioned
environs; ideas are expressed, above all, by means germane
to a particular historical situation. The historian is not so
much concerned with the actual presentation of ideas or the
way in which ideas find expression as with their substance,
their inner core, their essence. It is true that the idea of the
supremacy of the law originally stemmed from the anthropo-
morphic-allegorical interpretation of the relations between
soul and body, but this was merely the medieval application
of an ancient Hellenistic theme, presented, it is true, in a
Christian garb, a point which should not, however, hinder our
realizing its profound universal significance. For this allegory
of soul and body served as the bridge between the ancient and
the modern world—it was the intermediary expressing itself
in contemporary medieval terminology which filled the
Hellenistic shell with appropriate contents. This allegory
must be seen against the strong undercurrent of legal, philosophic, and also theological discussion of the idea of justice.
There is hardly a tract, arenga, gloss, or other work that did
not in one way or another deal with the idea of justice, which
thereby received precision: and this idea of justice was based

upon Christian cosmology, of which the law was no more than a crisp and readily comprehensible distillation. Behind the law stood justice and, stripped of all its paraphernalia, there was no other item which was of so crucial concern to medieval doctrine as justice. Although the contents of justice may vary, it was within the precincts of the descending theme of government and law that, as far as the Western orbit goes, this idea received its fullest and most comprehensive treatment. When James Madison declared that "Justice is the end of government. It is the end of civil society. It ever has been, and ever will be, pursued until it be obtained, or until liberty be lost in the pursuit," he expressed in pithy language a principle of distinguished medieval ancestry.[89] And when the same Madison attacked what he called "the impious doctrine in the old world" because according to it "the people were made for kings, not kings for the people," he reiterated in virtually identical language what—unbeknown to him—had already been denounced in the Middle Ages by Dante.[90]

Precisely because law, in order to be law, was to be based upon justice, it was conceived as the soul of the body corporate: and because the soul was held to be immortal, the law itself also was perceived as permanent. The sempiternity of the idea of law as the one and only regulating force within a body corporate—translating the abstract idea of justice into concrete terms of the law—raised the law to a basic principle which impressed itself upon the Middle Ages and far beyond. The respect for, if not the sanctity of, the law was the presupposition for orderly public government and social life. It was the law that was held to have infused permanency, stability, and sempiternity to the body politic; it was the law which breathed life into a public body. If peace were to

---

[89] See *The Federalist*, ed. Benjamin Fletcher Wright (Cambridge, Mass., 1961), no. 51, p. 358.

[90] *Ibid.*, no. 45, p. 325. For Dante's view see above, p. 135 n. 72.

obtain, the law was to be the foundation of any civilized form of government. The purely external way in which this profound idea was expressed—that is, the allegory of soul and body—was a historical contingency, but the idea itself has survived its medieval formulation and appears under different guises and different nomenclatures. It still is today the central issue of any civilized government.[91] The eve of the American Revolution furnishes a rather clear instance of how much this idea of the law as the soul of the body politic was in the minds of alert contemporaries and was, in fact, expressed in a manner not at all dissimilar to that of the Middle Ages. John Dickinson in 1774 had this to say:

> The *soul*, speaking of the *constitution*, has a right to prevent, or to relieve, any mischief to the *body* of the society, and to keep it in the best of health.[92]

Secondly, as a result of the liberalizing Aristotelian-Thomist themes and their concomitant concentration upon the individual and the citizen, subsequent intellectual efforts were directed toward the individual rights of the citizens, an outcome which I think was the logical and necessary complementary development of the idea of the supremacy of the law. It was the theory of the natural rights of man which gave its imprint to political and legal philosophy down to the eighteenth century—natural rights, that is, with which man was born and which were not the result of a specific grant by superior authority. The link between the natural law and the natural rights might well be seen to lie in the

[91] From the purely historical point of view it would seem, therefore, that the idea of the supremacy of law, of the rule of law or of the *Rechtsstaat,* should be kept apart from the form of government or its underlying ideology (i.e., royal, aristocratic, democratic, ascending or descending, communist or capitalist, et cetera). It is only in relation to what has been termed the theory of right law (*Lehre vom richtigen Recht*) that the two begin to show interdependence.

[92] John Dickinson, *An Essay on the constitutional power of Great Britain over the Colonies in America* (Philadelphia, 1774), p. 36.

Thomist stress of man's right reason (*recta ratio*), which was in course of time to free itself from the restrictions by which it was originally enveloped. It was the shift of emphasis from an objectively considered law to a subjectively perceived right which was the hallmark of this development. That the individual himself, man as a natural being, thereby came more and more to the fore seems self-evident. Man's humanity was raised to its pivotal function, with the consequence that primary value was attributed to the individual and only secondary importance to society, a not inconsiderable shift when compared with the situation in the high Middle Ages, soaked as it was with Platonic ideas. Man's right reason became the key with which the secrets of orderly, civilized, peaceful social life could be unlocked.[93] The natural rights of man, discoverable by right reason, emerged in the political field as the fundamental rights of the citizen.

My third observation concerns the application of the point which I have repeatedly tried to convey in these lectures, namely that if a theory is to make an impact, the historic presuppositions for its adoption must be favorable. This reflection appears to me to have particular relevance to my topic, for the theory of natural rights of man, with its necessary adjunct of the compact and consent theory, fell on fertile soil which feudal civilization had prepared for its adoption. It is at this juncture that the potent feudal practice with its offspring, the common law, came to assume its historic role, because the feudally inspired common law had already ascribed a number of fundamental rights to the individual. Can one then really wonder that the natural rights thesis was so readily accepted where feudal government had cultivated the ground? Once more, a statement of John Dickinson

---

[93] It is perhaps interesting to see that some English lawyers, for instance, Saint German, preferred the term "law of reason" to the "law of nature"; see Paul Vinogradoff, "Reason and Conscience in sixteenth-century Jurisprudence," *Law Quarterly Review*, XXIV (1909), 373ff.

on the eve of the American Revolution breathes, if I may say so, a truly medieval, that is, Bractonian spirit:

> The freedom of a people consists in being governed by laws in which no alteration can be made without their consent.[94]

It was the fusion or confluence of what might well be called feudal civilization and common law practice with the natural rights theories[95] which not only produced the Declaration of 1776, but also accounted for the steady constitutional development leading to democratic evolution. The American colonists had, so to speak, transferred from their native soil principles of government which were firmly rooted in medieval feudal practice. There is, to my mind, a direct lineage from Locke back to the feudal compact and consent in the Middle Ages and forward to the Declaration of Independence. "Locke did not need to convince the colonists because they had long been convinced, and they were already convinced because they had long been living under governments which did, in a rough and ready way, conform to the kind of government for which Locke furnished a reasoned foundation."[96] I might add that the gov-

---

[94] Dickinson, *Essay on Constitutional Power*, p. 113. See Bracton's statement that the laws can neither be modified nor destroyed without the common consent of all those with whose counsel and consent they have been promulgated; cited in Ullmann, *Principles of Government*, p. 177. Richard Bland, another pamphleteer, in his *The Colonel Dismounted*, had to say very much the same: he declared that under an English government men "are only subject to laws with their own consent and cannot be deprived of the benefit of these laws without a transgression of them"; quoted in Baylin, *Pamphlets*, p. 319.

[95] This might possibly explain Camden's statement that the law of nature was engrafted into the British constitution.

[96] Carl L. Becker, *The Declaration of Independence* (2d ed.; New York, 1942), p. 72. See further Friedrich, *The Philosophy of Law*, p. 32: Locke "rationalized views immanent in English legal and constitutional development in terms of the prevailing philosophic notions of natural law as they had developed on the Continent." See also Gottfried Dietze, *The Federalist: A Classic of Federalism and Free Government* (Baltimore, repr. 1965), pp. 324ff. For the influence of Samuel Pufendorf and John Wise on early revolutionary thought in America, see the excellent observations of Welzel, *Naturrecht*, pp. 156ff.

ernment for which Locke supplied the theory was in its essentials the heir of a government originally based on feudal law, principles, and practice and the feudal contract.[97] On the other hand, where feudal practice was wanting, where feudal government did not strike roots or advance, and where it remained stunted and atrophied, as in Germany, France, and Russia, there remained only the pure theory of the natural rights of man and the purely doctrinaire thesis of the people's sovereignty. Basic historical presuppositions were wanting for the smooth transition from the medieval subject status to the citizens' fundamental-natural rights. The attempted translation of theory into practice produced instability of governments, insecurity of the individual, and if pressed vigorously enough, led to armed insurrection and revolution. It is, I think, no paradox to say that in the Declaration of Independence there was a happy fusion of practice and ideology, each of which had a distinguished medieval ancestry—and this in a country which itself had no roots in the medieval past. "The philosophy of the Declaration was not taken from the French. It was not even new, but good old English doctrine newly formulated to meet a present emergency."[98] To this extent, then, the United States is the rightful heir of the European Middle Ages.

[97] The link between the common law and natural inalienable rights was indeed pointed out by some pamphleteers before the Revolution; see Baylin, *Pamphlets,* pp. 50ff.; see also Richard Bland in *ibid.,* p. 320.

[98] Becker, *The Declaration of Independence,* p. 79.

INDEX

Aachen, Council of, 23 *note* 46
Accusatorial principle, 93–94
Agricultural population, 22, 55–56, 85
Alan of Lille, 105 *note* 6, 113 *note* 28, 125 *note* 49
Albericus de Rosciate, 38 *note* 83, 39 *note* 86, 40 *note* 87, 89
Albertano de Brescia, 107–8
Albert the Great, 114–15, 120 *note* 39
Amercement, 20, 32
American Constitution, 68
American Revolution, 19 *note* 40, 148, 150. *See also* Declaration of Independence
Anacletus, 9 *note* 8
Anatomy, 113, 115
Anglo-Norman laws, 21. *See also Leges Henrici Primi*
Anglo-Saxon laws, 21, 28 *note* 60
Anima-corpus allegory, 46–49 *passim*, 146
Anointing. *See* Unction, royal
Anonymity, writers and artists, 32–33
Anthropology, medieval, 116 *note* 33
Aquinas. *See* Thomas Aquinas
Aristotle: effect in thirteenth century, 114; on Albert the Great, 115; on Dante, 113; on Giles of Rome, 139; on Thomas Aquinas, 122–23; translated, 119; and thesis of citizenship, 117–19, 130, 148
Arles, Council of, 23 *note* 46
Armils, royal, 29
Art, medieval, 32, 33, 44–45, 104–6, 112, 117, 121
Ascending theme of government and law, 56, 81, 88, 121, 137, 145. *See also* Rights, individual

Assizes, possessory, 86
Augustine, of Hippo, influence, 8 *note* 6, 12, 14, 22 *note* 44, 38 *note* 80, 46 *note* 98, 118, 144

Bacon, Roger, 112–13
Baldus de Ubaldis, 39 *note* 85, 40 *note* 89, 83 *note* 43, 84
Baptism, effects in public field, 7, 12, 101, 105, 111, 115, 123–24, 128
Bartolus of Sassoferrato, 139
Beamtenstaat, 90
Benevolentia, royal, 20. *See also* Grace, royal
Bible: influence in Middle Ages, 10–11, 23 *note* 45, 25 *note* 53, 28, 55, 121 *note* 41, 129; interpretation, 137–38; vernacular, 106 *note* 7, 144. *See also* Pauline conceptions
Bishop, murder of, 28
Blackstone, William, 92 *note* 59, 97
Bland, Richard, 150 *note* 94
Boniface VIII, 129–30
Boso of Burgundy, 19 *note* 39
Boucher, Jonathan, 19 *note* 40
Bracton, Henry de, 79, 150
Bulgarus, 39
Byzantium. *See* Constantinople

Cabillon, Council of, 24 *note* 50
Cambridge University, 92, 93, 95
Camden, William, 150 *note* 95
Canon law: medieval, 13, 16 *note* 32, 61, 73, 78, 85, 91–92, 96; modern, 8 *note* 5, 12 *note* 18, 31 *note* 67
Canterbury, school of, 11
Cardinal virtues, 124–25

153

THE INDIVIDUAL AND SOCIETY IN THE
MIDDLE AGES

by WALTER ULLMANN

Designer: Cecilie Smith
Typesetter: Monotype Composition Company, Inc.
Typeface: Fairfield and Perpetua
Printer: The Maple Press
Paper: Warren Olde Style
Binder: Moore & Company, Inc.